Policing

Policing

Adrian Kinnanc

Nelson-Hall nh Chicago

Library of Congress Cataloging in Publication Data

Kinnane, Adrian.
  Policing.

  Bibliography: p.
    1. Police   I. Title.
  HV7921.K56   363.2   78-26314
  ISBN 0-88229-327-3

Manufactured in the United States of America

10   9   8   7   6   5   4   3   2   1

Contents

Preface

Anyone who, in these days of information overload, seeks the attention of the reading public should explain what his message adds to the current state of knowledge about the subject at hand.

Believing that honest statements are often brief, I will state simply that I wrote this book because three years ago I felt terrible. A graduate student in clinical psychology, I felt terrible because I was bored and because my explorations of humanity were more often than not explorations of the theories of others about circumscribed aspects of human behavior. I felt I was missing something—some experiential component in my studies more "exciting" perhaps than the experiences of mental health clinics and psychiatric wards.

The decision to join a police department was a product of my fantasies at the time. These fantasies were telling me that there was more to be learned on the streets than in office settings. The more I read of the police literature available, the more I was convinced that first-hand police experience was essential to an understanding of police and their work. So I finished my formal coursework (postponing my doctoral research for a time) and joined the police department. My commitment was totally open-ended (that is, I didn't know if or when I would ever leave) and I was not considered unusual by the department except for my abnormal number of graduate credits. I honestly thought—though perhaps I *had* to think it at the time—that I might make a career of police work, picking up my Ph.D. from within the department or working some other arrangement out with the University. The future obviously did not concern me much at the time. I only knew that policing was something I wanted to do and experience from the inside out.

The transition from a high-pressure graduate school program to an urban police academy was not easy. But by the end of four months of seemingly interminable instruction, I waited eagerly with my friends for assignment to a district.

I was eventually assigned to an operations squad, which gave me experience in foot and cruiser patrol (evening shift), cruiser patrol (daywork), strike duty, plainclothes details, and other special assignments. Things went fine for several months, until I faced up to the fact that I was again feeling terrible.

This time I felt terrible about a host of things having to do with the public, my fellow officers, the department, the profession, the criminal justice system, and mankind in general. But there were things I felt good about, too. I had learned from men whose courage, tact, and kindness were often touching in their simplicity. I had experienced the many satisfactions that come from good policing, and, to be honest, I felt I had earned the respect and friendship of men whose standards and judgments are often harsh. And I had done this as a police officer, not as an identified "student" or "professor-in-uniform."

But while there were many good things, there were also many things that were shoved under the rug, not articulated and, worse, not even acknowledged. I felt that there was a wide chasm of misunderstanding between the world I had known before policing and the world I had come to know as an officer.

Prior to my interest in street patrol, I had subscribed to the usual educated-liberal stereotypes of cops as rigid and dull authoritarians. Six years in the Army National Guard (1970-1976) as a military policeman did nothing to change these stereotypes and made it even more difficult for me to dig through the military appearance of policing to the complexities underneath. When I felt I had succeeded in reaching these realities, I wanted to do something to help others understand what their police really do and the circumstances under which they do it.

In the final balance, police work as such was not as interesting to me as clinical psychology. And while it might be possible for a clinical psychologist to involve himself with policing, it would be next to impossible for an uncredentialed police officer to work as a clinical psychologist. Moreover, there is often an attitude against nontechnical innovation in police departments, and street officers are not expected or encouraged to work or think beyond the rather narrow confines of the police tradition.

I felt as though I could make a contribution towards citizens' understanding of police, and felt that this contribution could be made more effectively if I were not professionally obligated to the department. In addition, I grew restless in the department, unused as I was to stifling criticisms, suggestions, and questions about my environment.

I also felt terrible about resigning, however much I realized that it was probably best for me to do so. Even over the course of one year I had built up working relationships of which I was proud. Policing affords opportunities for adventure, loyalty, comradeship-under-fire (both figurative and real), and pride that few other professions can offer. Police demand these qualities from one another, and if one can measure up—for whatever length of time—the feelings of accomplishment and belonging are hard to relinquish.

For over a year after my resignation, and even after I received my Ph.D., I experienced intense nostalgia whenever I passed a patrolman. It was the nostalgia of the former "insider" who was now outside. The calls coming over the radio, the knowledge of the dramas being played out behind the droll codes, the constant challenge to guard one's territory and to measure up for one's squad—all this filled me with a great longing to return to patrol. For over two years after I resigned, I had vivid dreams of rejoining and policing again—of being in the roll call room, of putting on the uniform, of searching fields and buildings for robbery suspects, and the like. The dreams were so real that for a few moments after waking I would wonder what it was I actually did for a living. It became clear to me that leaving the department was as difficult as joining.

I like to think that this book says a lot of what my former colleagues would say if they had access to a publisher. There are many things about their work which they intuit and respond to but do not clearly spell out for themselves or for others. I feel that spelling these things out can enable all of us—police and citizens—to cooperate in our mutual law enforcement responsibilities.

I have presented observations, assessments, and schemas, but I have presented some strong opinions as well. This habit I learned from my former colleagues. Their honesty and bluntness were contagious, and a participant-observer analysis of patrol work would be incomplete if not touched by these qualities.

Finally, I have changed names in my illustrations and have deliberately failed to identify my department. It is not as important to identify names or locations as it is to understand that all urban police share common tasks and common pressures. Until greater trust and appreciation is aroused in the community, the existing differences between departments are not likely to make much difference in the daily work of the police officer.

CHAPTER 1

The Context
of Policing

FOUR OF US sat in the third row at her funeral. The City Baptist Church was warm on that June morning, and nurses in white sat attentively beside the older women. We did not know the dead woman and she had not known us. We had been given a set of ill-fitting white gloves at the station house and told that we were to be an honor guard at the funeral of a former school crossing guard.

The preacher was a distant relative of the deceased, and he gave a very moving performance of mixed sermon and song. The nurses looked nervous and fanned their perspiring charges as they heaved up cries of "Amen!" and "Oh Lord!" We were police officers and white. Everyone else was black. We were greeted and treated warmly. At the gravesite, a wiry old man who had had too much to drink began competing with the preacher in talking the woman into her grave. We stood awkwardly, fidgeting from one foot to another before someone finally shooed him away. Each of us placed a single red rose on the coffin to end the ceremony.

A few months earlier I had been part of another honor guard, this time at the Catholic funeral of a former Polish police sergeant. The church was in an ethnic ghetto of the city where

second and even third generations spoke both English and
Polish. The mass was in Polish, and the trip to the gravesite
wound through the dull wharves and dockyards of the southeast
part of town. After the burial there was a reception in the upstairs hall of a Polish social society. We sat at the back table
and ate cold-cut sandwiches in silence. We could not understand
what some of the people were saying and, with the exception of
one middle-aged woman who tried very hard, no one seemed to
know what to do with these cops at the back table. One of my
colleagues hung up his uniform coat and hat and ate with gusto
for a full half hour. I remember trying unsuccessfully to feel
hungry.

Another funeral came in April. A young police officer had
died after a month of transfusions and operations in a city hospital. He had been shot in the chest while responding to a disturbance call, and the newspapers had carried a poem written
by his wife as she and their two small children waited for the
worst. The poem was strong but resigned.

When he died, police departments from several states sent
contingents to the funeral. Many from the officer's own department went on their own time. Most had given blood to help
keep him alive. The funeral was a closed affair, but the pro-
cession to the cemetery was several miles long and there were
hundreds of people at the grave. I could not hear the eulogy.
Then someone played taps as the body was lowered and the
widow screamed.

I went home with a splitting headache and rested for a
couple of hours before the evening shift began.

I begin this chapter with three funerals not to be morbid
but to underscore the diversity of lives and customs in a modern
city. Our society, particularly our urban society, has many racial, ethnic, and generational subcultures all operating in a
rough equilibrium. We speak different languages and share different heritages. We are not a "melting pot" but a mosaic of
traditions, few of which are native to American soil.

Our police reflect this diversity. Departments are usually
staffed with members of the community. However, political
machinations in some of our major cities have biased police
selection in favor of certain ethnic groups—the Irish, for in-

stance—while on a national level, the FBI in the days of J. Edgar Hoover showed a marked preference for graduates of eastern Catholic men's colleges.

On the city level, police not only reflect the community's diversity but must deal with its complications as well. Our heterogeneity is a source of both mutual enrichment and hostility. Conflicts between groups of differing status, race, and political attitudes often confront police officers. This situation is aggravated by the fact that we have little in the way of substantive tradition and custom to guide us.[1] Our commitment to at least the spirit of classic democracy means that atypical, heretical, non-conformist, or just plain different points of view have some chance of surviving attempts to quash them. And our tolerance, perhaps even reverence, for change, innovation, and novelty means that our values and environments are usually in a constant state of flux. Most of us, for instance, have had the experience of going to a store we have not been to in a while only to find that it is closed, has been torn down, or has been changed into something else. There may even be an entirely different structure on the site.

We give our children a great deal of latitude while growing up to "be what they want to be," although the results of their experimentations and wanderings often disturb us. Things that we consider fundamental to society's well-being—such as marriage, parenthood, family, church, the work ethic, and schooling —are re-examined by our children and often found wanting. This makes us worry for the future, though we usually fail to recognize the insecurity and discomfort such experimentation causes in the youngsters themselves.

Police departments have always responded to societal diversity in an intuitive, unsophisticated way. It is characteristic of police, as it is of all of us, that we deal with complex phenomena by forcing them into simpler categories and applying existing solutions or explanations. This is changing. For example, a Maryland suburb north of Washington, D.C., had experienced a large influx of Spanish-speaking people. Storeowners in the area began to complain of an increase in shoplifting, and police found themselves arresting a large number of Hispanic people for this crime. A study was commissioned to explore the situation. The study concluded that the Hispanics were merely following the custom of their native countries in which one goes to market with a large shopping bag, puts one's goods in the bag, and pays on the way out. Such behavior in this American suburb constituted a "criminal intent to conceal" goods and made the unfortunate shoppers liable to arrest. Language difficulties, fear of police, and a patrolman's natural inclination to associate poverty with larceny prevented the explanation from surfacing earlier. Once correctly analyzed, the situation was easily resolved through educative measures and publicity.

The idea of a diverse and active country carries with it the idea of *change*. Since its inception in a spirit of revolution, America has experienced a rate of growth and change so accelerative and encompassing that Alvin Toffler has called it "future shock." This accelerated growth made it possible for waves of immigrants to populate our cities and create the cultural mosaic we have just described. Though these immigrants came primarily from Europe, many came from our own South. Most came to the same places—our cities—for the same reasons. Almost all wanted a change. Some worked for it, some were caught up in it, and some had to fight for it. With some, the desire and the struggle continue.

Change, of course, occurs on many levels, of which ethnic grouping is only one. Change is a facet of individual behavior, regardless of group affiliation, and here as well we tend to simplify complexity and slow down change by cramming a lot of information into a few categories. Another way of saying this is that we "stereotype" people. This is a perfectly natural and useful process that is harmful only insofar as it shades into unfair judgments, a denial of rights, or a vehicle for hate.

Most of us stereotype others, though we remain for the most part flexible enough to alter our conclusions when new evidence arrives. For instance, what is your reaction to the word "doctor"? And what is your reaction to the word "wino"? You probably have two very different sets of associations to these concepts, the former largely positive and the latter largely negative. But suppose I can show you a wino who was a good doctor before alcoholism ruined his career and his family? Suppose I can show you a doctor who is a wife-beater, a child-molester, an embezzler, or even a murderer? And conversely, suppose I can show you a wino who reads philosophy texts between binges, or prays fervently to God in his hopelessness, or cries silently to himself in a park because he has no one to turn to?

A police officer sees, as few other professionals do, some common threads of good and weakness running through all of us.[2] He forms his own stereotypes, or working assumptions, but they are probably not like yours or mine. He picks them up informally in his acculturation to the police group and in his own experience. He seldom has reason or cause to articulate them, and he often wonders why his being a police officer gradually alienates him from former friends and contacts. He wonders just who is right and who is wrong about the human condition, but he does it inside himself, unaided by counsel and often without the benefit of any clear sense of what is happening to him.

It is this violent rocking back and forth between differing assumptions, false predictions, confirmed pessimisms, surprising optimisms, and shattered generalities that helps make the officer cynical. The price he pays for his own personal safety and effectiveness often is a sense of balance and proportion in his attitudes towards those he polices. Thus it is practically dogma among street policemen that the only thing one can expect is the unexpected.[3]

We should not leave the subject of change without discussing the conservative nature of policing. It is often said that police are against change, that they are reactionary, or even that those who created and defined the police role did so to preserve their own investments and prevent the forces of change from eroding the status quo.

It is true that police departments screen for those applicants who do, in fact, seem to be against change in many of the shakier aspects of our morality (drugs, marijuana, sexual permissiveness, pornography). The rationale is that someone who does not feel personally that present legislation is proper cannot be counted on to enforce laws which, however questionable, are nonetheless on the books. The answer to the problem of enforcing unpopular or even unreasonable laws ("blue laws," for instance) has been to find police officers who are (or who know enough to say they are) comfortably religious, defiantly heterosexual, and appropriately punitive toward moral deviants.

It has been my experience that police officers are more competent and more responsible than their superiors often assume. I feel that they are capable of separating private judgments from official duty, and that were they allowed to consider the complexities of many of our laws they could provide valuable perspectives on moral behavior to their legislatures. The present system serves more to shield the department from embarrassment than to aid in the evolution of viable and enforceable laws.

Certain "victimless crimes" such as gambling and homosexuality are gradually becoming legitimate, even to the point of states establishing their own lotteries, for example. But until the active debate around these questions resolves itself in some form of legislation, the police function will involve duties that the individual officer may or may not agree with. (The enforcement element of the police function will always be heavy-handed until the discretionary nature of his work is openly acknowledged. But more of this in the following chapters.) I would only add that in many police departments, selection seems aimed at finding applicants who will never question the conventional wisdom. This is unrealistic as a goal and unfair to the officers who may be thrown into unconventional waters.

Related to the theme of change is America's attitude toward *authority*. As a people we are profoundly ambivalent toward authority of all kinds. This includes police authority but extends to political, military, parental, school, religious, and professional authority as well. It is commonly acknowledged that for better or worse "official" authority of all sorts has been eroded in recent times. But it is less often acknowledged that other authority has been abdicated as well as eroded.

This is probably more true of parental authority than of any other type and explains why Dr. Benjamin Spock, a major advocate of "permissive" child-rearing, has been blamed for many of our woes. At a time when children were most in need of proper authority (churches and schools having been undercut by the mobility and "nuclearity" of the modern family), Dr.

Spock seemed to encourage parental abdication. This is not actually so, but it is a popular interpretation that shows people's sensitivity to the loss of control in American families.

Any single explanation or interpretation of our attitudes toward authority is bound to miss the mark. It is a complex question which deserves a complex answer. Suffice it to say that a uniformed police officer is a highly visible symbol of authority and thus becomes a focal point for all sorts of fantasies, resentments, and angers. The fantasies he stimulates are more often than not those of hostility, omnipotence, and violence. The resentments and angers he arouses can range from the mildly irritated to the murderous. It is probably the rare person in our society who does not feel negatively toward the police on some level, even if these negative feelings are mixed with awe, respect, or gratitude.[4]

Police are often considered a necessary evil whose control should be limited, whose organization should be fragmented and local, and whose numbers should be minimal.[5] We have even coined the term "police state" to represent all that is contrary to our political and social ideals. Thus in our society there are over forty thousand local law enforcement departments, excluding federal and other regulatory agencies. Most of these departments are the small-town type consisting only of a chief and a handful of officers. It was not until the 1830s that a rising crime rate forced reluctant citizens to organize city police departments on a large scale.

Police were created in ambiguity and were expected to keep a tolerable level of social control without alienating the "better sort" of hard-working taxpayer. This ambiguity rises every time one of us receives a traffic ticket and mutters, "Why isn't he out catching crooks instead of harassing decent citizens (like me)?" We have never been able to decide whether our police are an instrument of general social order or a means of controlling lower-class, poor, immigrant, black, or otherwise "bothersome" groups.

Our romantic characterizations of law enforcers (the frontier sheriff or the "private eye") clearly segregate "good guys" from "bad guys". The consequent expectation by the public that police can see who is good and who is bad leads to continual misunderstandings and disappointments. The hostility generated by these disappointments leads many people to associate police with a certain lower-class degeneracy. They become dirtied by their contacts with outcast groups. This means that even the most cursory confrontation with a policeman "taints" the offended citizen as well. His need to dissociate himself from the "criminal element", from the officer, from the sloppy and messy criminal justice system for which he feels no personal need or responsibility, and from his own misbehavior.[6]

Police are thus given power to enforce all laws in even-handed fashion but must adapt to a reality that tells them otherwise. It is the tacit understanding of large segments of the community that the police are not supposed to take their jobs *too* seriously, unless of course the objects of their activity are the usual outcast groups. (One of the largest and most troublesome outcast groups, by the way, consists of the teenage children of these "special" people. In this case they want the police to act, but they want to have the final say. Thus we have a juvenile court and probation system specifically designed to short-circuit the criminal justice process.) The police naturally resent being used as instruments in personal and familial battles.

If whites react negatively to police authority, blacks almost explode.[7] We are all familiar with the history of slavery and legalized discrimination in the United States and it is not hard for us to understand why blacks react angrily to police authority. But without disputing any of the legitimate and amply documented causes of black anger, we should look at some other facts of interracial life in America to interpret black attitudes toward police and vice-versa. It may be important not only to recognize but perhaps to legitimize police anger at blacks, just as we have legitimized black anger at police, in order to understand the realities of policing a "ghetto" neighborhood. Because this issue is so important and complex, it will be dealt with in a separate chapter of this book.

Another national attitude that deserves attention is our proclivity for guns and *violent conflict resolution*. Here too we are deeply ambivalent, professing ideals of non-violence, teamwork, and cooperation, yet feasting on movies, TV shows, and novels constructed almost wholly on violent themes. Boys especially come to feel that there is an equation of masculinity and destructive potential. Many of our poorer neighborhoods are very cruel and violent places in which to live because of this equation. The more obvious forms of violence evident in our cities arouse fear in the suburbs and in middle-class neighborhoods (of whatever race), and citizens arm themselves in alarming numbers. Large sums of federal money are spent annually on "summer job" and make-work programs for uneducated, marginally employable, lower-class teenage males just to keep them off the streets and give them some pocket money they would otherwise presumably steal.

Most children are fascinated by a policeman's openly-worn "real gun," since they have been shooting at their surroundings with toy guns for as long as they can remember. They often ask whether or not the officer has ever shot anyone, and their bright-eyed expectancy is, I must confess, a trifle upsetting. Upsetting too (gun-toting parents take note!) is their eagerness to hold the revered object "for just a little bit."[8]

Military veterans occasionally discuss the merits of a .45 calibre vs. a .38 calibre revolver, trying to rekindle an old spark of armed excitement that died in cold wars and prosperity. And many adolescent boys know more about the specifications of high-powered police cruiser engines than do the officers themselves.

This fascination for violence which, in much popular literature and cheap films, focuses on the police becomes a fascination for police work which attracts as many "police buffs" to police as it does police applicants to policing. There is a mystique about "the cops"—that their lives are intense, dangerous, and exciting, that their love lives are torrid and active, that they are tough and hard-bitten yet understanding and heroic—that continues to attract wide audiences.

We are, after all, conflicted about *pleasure* as well. On the one hand we drive ourselves hard, achieving enormous heights of technological and material sophistication. This is the heritage of Puritanism in American morality—the work ethic of self-denial and the postponement of gratification. What we have lost, however, is the world-view of the Puritan, the conviction that God controls our destinies and rewards those who sacrifice and obey. And while the Puritans were never quite as puritanical as we usually think, they at least had some relatively consistent system of values to define life and give it purpose and perspective.

Those of us adhering to some moral and ethical framework find that framework increasingly inadequate in the face of such issues as genetic research, abortion, neutron weaponry, homosexuality, adolescent sex, and even crime and punishment. These issues push us into a gray world of moral decisions where we are guided only by vestiges of basic moral principles and some lonely feelings of decency and good will. In the decision vacuum that accompanies weak valuation, the temptation to do "what feels good" becomes strong. But this desire clashes with ingrained habits of self-discipline and self-reproach to lend a uniquely explosive flavor to our pleasure-seeking. A work pace that cannot be slacked will be chemically destroyed at a crowded bar or a noisy party. Empty moments will be narcotized by televised athletic combat, or compulsive sex, or compulsive gambling, or compulsive shopping. The consumption of goods is a national pastime at which we are unexcelled among nations. If dispositions are less benign, fighting and the infliction of pain may be used to goad a bored lover or relative into action. And the policeman, occasionally suffering from the same malaise, will be called to restore a false and unsatisfactory peace.

Because our poor suffer not so much from self-denial as from simple denial, their conflicts tend to be externalized. They are not as guilty about being bored as they are simply bored. The dominant motif among the poor is not anger and resentment, as many assume. These are predominantly the emotions of the frustrated middle class. The poor are more often apathetic, defeated, and resigned. Thus their violence assumes a gratuitous, random character that is highly frightening to the middle class, whose violence, if ugly, is at least purposive in a goading or object-arousing sense. Witness, for example, the looting which occurred during New York City's twenty-five-hour electrical blackout in July 1977. Thirty-five hundred people—mostly young black and Hispanic males—were arrested. Not only did the extent of the damage shock observers, but the seeming "party" atmosphere surrounding the looting baffled most people. Whether this behavior needs to be explained in sociological terms or not, it remains true that it frightens people who have little or no sense of the profound flatness and boredom spawned by poverty.

For the very apathetic and emotionally blunted, violence itself can assume the status of a goal. It can be one of life's simple pleasures, very directly and horribly enjoyed as an end in itself. While people of this bent are indeed dangerous, when their pursuit of aggression is combined with neurological impairment or psychosis they become real menaces to the community. Often our fears lead us to exaggerate the number of pathologically violent people on our streets. They are rare, though without more accurate diagnostic criteria and statistics it is difficult to be more than subjective in one's judgments. Suffice it to say that police officers see enough pathological violence in one year to alter permanently their conceptions of safety and security. One does not confront pointless sadism and walk away unaffected.

Still another of our conflicts centers on *youth*. While we glorify the benefits of youth and spend millions of dollars each year trying to "stay on the young side," we often fear our children and resent them. We have made adolescence such a difficult time for our youth that they have formed their own subculture, with shifting, trendy norms and "values" constructed as much to annoy adults as to guide behavior. Our mistrust and jealousy of teenagers is so great that we exclude them from the larger society years after they are capable of making meaningful contributions. Yet they are our children, and our guilt is enormous.

What this means to the police officer is this: as the enforcement agent in the criminal justice system, he is called upon *in loco parentis* to control the behavior of unruly adolescents. This generally involves arrest where a few words of warning will not do the trick (many children learn through experience that verbal warnings are meaningless). However, guilty Americans do not want youth punished too much. Therefore arrested juveniles are back on the street in no time at all, a little released in the custody of one or two usually ineffective parents

within a few hours of their arrest. Because police are so frequently used in this fashion, the backlog of cases for juvenile
court judges is staggering. There is great pressure to release all
but the most dangerous teenagers, and the great majority of
arrested juveniles are back on the street in no time at all, a little
more cop-wise, a little more cynical, a little more convinced
that society is as ineffectual as Mom and/or Dad. The lenient
treatment of juvenile offenders is a sore spot with police, for
here their personification of society's ambivalence becomes explicit and even institutionalized.[9] They feel caught in the middle,
"damned if they do and damned if they don't."[10]

We are, in addition to our other conflicts, more divided
than we care to admit about "freedom" and "equality" for our
citizens. What Gunnar Myrdal has called "the American dilemma," i.e., the presence of a slave-remnant population in a
political democracy, is a dilemma on a larger scale as well. For
ours is an intensely competitive society in which to the victors
go the spoils. We are really very unequal educationally, economically, and culturally, although the rest of the world may
indeed be in far worse shape. We maintain the myth that all
have an equal chance for success and that resulting differences
in achievement are due to motivational and genetic factors beyond our collective control. We often blind ourselves to the
considerable gaps between our ideals and our realities and to
the fact that we are often not what we profess to be.

Yet despite this, we are among the most egalitarian and
fair-minded people on earth. If we are naive in our assessment
of social injustices, we are equally naive in our zest for quick
solutions and remedies (such as the "war on poverty"). We
generally have the best of intentions and are perhaps more willing than we should be to "take the rap" for the failings of
citizens we have disappointed.

The police officer usually feels deeply that inequality is a
fact of life.[11] He also has rare first-hand knowledge of the aggregate personal and social factors that put a brake on achievement and make true freedom and equality at best idealistic
goals. It is therefore not surprising that a researcher found that
police rank "equality" lower on a list of values than did a
national sample of white males, and much lower than a na-

tional sample of black males.[12] This perspective of the police officer is often interpreted as prejudice or bigotry, resulting from a combination of ignorance and insensitivity to human need. Others willingly project their own hostilities and prejudices onto the police, seeking safety in the knowledge that the forces of law and order are working to insulate them from contact with despised groups.

As a rookie officer, I was for several months startled by the readiness with which some white people would express to me their negative feelings towards "niggers" and "those animals." At first I thought that I was simply a safe audience for such expressions, i.e., I was considered to share those feelings and would not take offense. But after a while I got the feeling that these people were looking to tap some reservoirs of hate in me, to be reassured that the powers of the law were cognizant of the fact that blacks are the root of all crime. This was part of it. They also were frightened, confused people who wanted to hear that everything was under control. If you suspend judgment about these people and let them talk, you often find that their confusion and fear transcend race. They want stability and comfort and security, and feel that an impersonal and threatening world is about to pull the rug out from under them at any moment. By letting their small-minded remarks about blacks pass by, you force them to look deeper into themselves.

If the police officer is prejudiced against blacks (or Puerto Ricans, or other minorities), his prejudgments are usually based on the realities of inner-city survival, not the vague fears and hates of the suburbs.

We have seen that it may be very difficult to define the role of police in a society as deeply divided as ours is on such police-relevant issues as authority, morality, violence, change, youth, and equality. Police crave acceptance and esteem but find that no role is adequate to satisfy our polyglot needs. Their labors frequently earn them little reward and much hardship. However, while we might speculate on what the police role should be, the police are, as usual, working on the streets of our society defining that role in countless decisions and actions.

CHAPTER 2

The Police Function

"The development of a fully reasoned meaning of the police role in society that might give rise to a range of rationally methodological work procedures, must be worked out from within the occupation, it cannot be imparted to it by outsiders."

Egon Bittner[9]

JUST AS OUR society is complex, so policing it is complex and riddled with contradictions. On the most abstract level, policing is primarily a reactive function masquerading as a proactive one. Police do not fight crime nearly as much as they clean up after it. The job is structured in such a way that the appearance of pro-action is maintained, but the basic function is still reactive. For instance, if an officer tells you that he has been "patrolling his post" for an hour (proactive), this often means that he has had no calls for service and little to do. But of course he cannot appear idle, so the language he employs, or is taught to employ, gives the appearance of work.

In reality, the officer's eight hours of duty are rarely idle because police administrators have seen to it that officers have more than a proactive language to show city councils and taxpayers. Here is where we encounter the touchy issue of "quotas." No police administrator in the country (who wishes to remain

15

at his job) will assert that a quota system is operative in his department. Administrators do not like the word because it leaves them in a legally untenable position.[1] But the reality is that a rough "level of production" is required of every patrol officer in several major categories every month. (The specific number and types of categories might vary from department to department.) These most often include parking tickets, moving violations, car stops (investigative), bank and business checks, and arrests (felony and misdemeanor). Occasionally an officer will be told by his sergeant to "get your stats up" (statistics). This is generally a strong hint (normally not required because all officers understand the system very well) that a man is not pulling his share of the squad's work. And of course the only reason the sergeant cares, unless he is trying to drive the man out of his squad or force him to resign for some reason, is that someone higher in the bureaucracy than himself will put pressure on him if his squad's totals fall below last year's average. Everyone must pull his weight to maintain good relations with the sergeant—the most important person in the patrolman's working life.

An officer with fifteen years on the force was told by his sergeant one day to "get his stats up." "Jake," said the sergeant, "there's a rumor going around here that you just might lock someone up today." The informal order to make an arrest was coated with humor to ward off bad feelings, but the message got through. Jake remembered the name of a teenage boy he knew who had called him a "mother-fuckin' pig" the previous day from a safe distance. He sat down in the roll call room, filled out a juvenile custody sheet (the juvenile equivalent of an arrest form) without actually arresting the boy, and took it down to the boy's house where his mother signed it. That finished the matter, and Jake went back to his job. Through a combination of bureaucratic finesse and ingenuity on Jake's part and a lenient system for processing juvenile offenders on society's part, the boy was arrested and released to his mother without even knowing it. In the time it takes to arrest one adult, transport him to jail, and fill out incident reports, arrest forms, and a statement of charges, an officer can arrest and release to parental custody nearly five juveniles (barring complications). And the statistics reflect only the gross numbers, not "five juveniles throwing stones at cars" or "one adult, aggravated assault."

Several elements besides the "onward and upward" production ethic of bureaucracies are involved in the police administrator's effort to give policing a proactive veneer. And these elements are, not by chance, those elements which divide street police from administrators ("the brass downtown") to such a great degree. For the mistrust and animosity between beat officers and the brass (who, incidentally, have usually spent many years on the street themselves) are enormous.

The first element is the attitude on the part of administrators that "the crime is out there—it's happening, so don't tell us you can't find it because we know it's there." Car stops offer a good example of how a genuinely proactive patrol procedure —the stopping of suspicious vehicles for stolen checks—becomes a falsely proactive one. Forms called "car stop sheets" are issued to police officers on which they record a maximum of six stopped cars (license number, time and location stopped, operator's name and address, and any unusual characteristics of the vehicle) in one eight-hour shift before using another form. Because three car stops are recorded on the front of the form and three on the back, the back three wind up being "bonus stops" that show extra effort on the officer's part. Every officer on patrol (i.e., not on special assignment) is expected to bring in three car stops per shift in this department. This is the unofficial "quota" he must meet in order to pull his weight in the squad and gain the sergeant's approval. Only an exceptionally busy night, involving several calls for service or some other time-consuming activity (e.g., a homicide call), will excuse an officer from bringing in his car stops, although he can overproduce on one day to make up for unproductive days.

Anyone who thinks it is easy to spot three "suspicious" vehicles in eight hours should try doing it. It is frequently impossible to come up with a sufficient number of "quality car stops" (three or more juveniles in an easily stolen car—a '62 Chevy or a '66 Pontiac, for example—driving in an appropriately suspicious manner) within the time and other limits of an eight-hour tour. But "the crime is out there—it's up to you to find it." Were this possible, police officers would do it. They are resourceful and usually quite persistent. But it is not always possible. Suspicious vehicles can be and are found, but not three times a day by every patrol officer on every shift in a district.

An officer pulled over a late model Chevelle with temporary tags occupied by three teenage males. When he asked to see the license and registration, the operator said disgustedly, "Sure, man. This is only the third time I've been stopped in the past hour!" Just in driving across town, this car had been stopped three times for a stolen check—a rare "quality car stop" that was being exploited consistently (and to the driver, irritatingly) by police of different districts.

Police fill their car stop sheets by several means. One is to record drivers and cars stopped for moving violations and safety repair orders (headlight or taillight out, cracked windshield, tires worn, and the like). Another, used by the more daring or cynical, is to record the license and registration information of friends and relatives to use as a "car stop reserve" on slow nights.

Late one night toward the end of the four-to-twelve shift, an officer observed a car speeding moderately down a main road. He took off in pursuit, intending to get one more car stop (not a moving violation) before the end of his shift. When the speeding car pulled over, the officer got out of his car and approached the driver's window. What followed was one of those awkward moments when an officer pulls over an off-duty officer driving his private car. "Oh," said the patrol officer. "Sorry I didn't see your uniform when you went by." "Careful—I'm armed," joked the traffic violator. The officer laughed and prepared to return to his patrol car when the off-duty man called out to him, "Hey, what do you need, a car stop or something?" The patrolman replied yes, and the man produced his license and registration to a grateful colleague.

A second element in constructing the proactive veneer is the traditional concept of law enforcers as "crime fighters." Most law enforcement agencies today define the police role as generally threefold:
1) the apprehension of criminals;
2) the prevention of crime;
3) protection of the public health and safety.

All three of these categories are basically proactive (proaction being determined on the basis not of who initiates police-citizen interaction but rather of what is done once the initial contact is made). The first and third are reasonably so, but the second is not. The police concept of crime prevention runs as follows. First, if a man goes to jail, he will not commit any crimes (of concern to the public) while he is incarcerated, so all the crimes he would have committed had he not been imprisoned are thus "prevented." Second, if an officer is alert, suspicious, and knowledgeable, he can make his territory uncomfortable for criminals and drive them to other areas. Theoretically, if all police everywhere were this vigilant, criminals would have nowhere to ply their trade and crime would cease. This is, of course, nonsense.

Police administrators respond sensitively to public pressures and conceptions of the police role. For in the final analysis, it is the citizenry which, through its allotment of tax money and use of the press, shapes the function of its police. The public— you and I—have put the entire responsibility for curbing criminal behavior on the police.[2] We have neglected to face the challenge of providing remedies for the social and personal conditions that produce crime and criminals. We find it far easier to view crime as the willful activity of a willfully immoral person, acting in sheer perversity and wickedness against our laws and mores. When the genesis of crime is seen in this light, we feel no need to "do something about it" because purposive anti-social behavior is a matter of the criminal's free will.[3] We therefore call on our police—who for the most part share our moralistic conception of criminality—to separate the wheat from the chaff while we wash our hands of the whole process.

Police know that crime prevention is largely impossible.[4] By carefully following patterns of specific crimes, such as auto thefts and burglaries, and by the skillful application of patrol tactics, an officer can occasionally prevent a person from committing a crime—that day. But he cannot prevent a person from wanting to commit a crime, and that is really what crime prevention is all about. And of course he can only react to such crimes of passion as murder, assault, rape, and impulsive vandalism when they occur in places inaccessible to his patrol. Moreover, one should keep in mind that for some people, such as adolescent auto thieves, compulsive shoplifters, and some vandals, the possibility of apprehension by the police only heightens the excitement and stimulation of anti-social behavior.

Police recognize explicitly their limited role in crime prevention, and they reinforce that limited role by believing that no one can prevent a person from wishing to break the law— one can only prevent that wish from materializing.[5] Police generally feel that efforts to rehabilitate criminals are a waste of time. Their role leads them to believe strongly in the virtues of punishment, and this belief makes the role of "crime fighter" an easier one to accept.

This conception of crime as a willful sign of moral decay underlies all the pressure for arrests and statistics. Every public outcry over increasing crime is inevitably followed by increased arrests for the relevant category of crime. The police produce the records of their arrests to show that they are "doing something" about the problem. Meanwhile the conditions that contributed to the increase in crime are never studied, or even acknowledged, and everyone is left with a nagging feeling that the whole problem is simply beyond control. The etiology of criminal behavior deserves a closer look.

A rookie officer's first impressions of a ghetto are memorable—or, rather, unforgettable. The crunch of ever-present broken glass (mostly discarded wine bottles broken by small children who either simply enjoy the sound or are trying to tell us something important about their feelings) beneath the cruiser's tires; the pungent odor of dog feces; the dried snot plastered on almost every kid's upper lip; the trash and garbage which routinely fill most alleys and corners; the smell of cooking grease; the palpable futility, frustration, and hostility which are masked by alcoholic giddiness on a Friday evening; the heavy incidences of mugging, assault, robbery, rape, and murder—how did this neighborhood ever get this way? Human passions are often released in the simplest way available, and thus police, reflecting the attitudes of the larger society, are quick to agree with any statement implying a gross equation between blacks and dirt, between blacks and crime.

What we are dealing with here is one of the fundamental issues of our time, with the most profound implications for our future. It is the "nature vs. nurture" or "heredity vs. environment" conflict. For our purposes, is a criminal a criminal by nature, a rotten apple beyond all salvation? Or is he a criminal because of the way he was brought up? And if he is a criminal because he had a bad childhood, neglectful or incompetent parents, and so forth, can that be changed?

As usual, the "truth" probably lies somewhere in between. A person may well be born with certain traits, such as stubbornness, passivity, or restlessness. But a lot of his behavior is also directly attributable to environmental contingencies. The real sticking point, however, is this: while conceding that certain types of environments lead to increased frequencies of certain behaviors, we insist on believing that *if a person really wants to,* he can change himself and overcome the handicap of a negative environment. If he is successful, we credit him with "strong character," and if he fails, we fault him for moral weakness or simple laziness.

Some behavioral psychologists maintain that we are "copping out" on our responsibilities to alter bad environments and thus decrease anti-social behavior. They maintain it is not so much the individual who must change himself but we who must change the conditions that determine individual behavior. There is a strong element of truth in this view, but I think the issue is a great deal more complex and far from ready resolution. It involves the transmission of cultural and subcultural behavior standards over which societal reformers may have little control.

An officer received a call to a five-and-dime store where a private security guard was holding two pre-teen black boys whom he had caught shoplifting some reflector kits for their bicycles. The officer put the boys in the back seat of his cruiser while the inevitable crowd gathered to goad him and urge the release of the boys. On his way to the station to fill out juvenile custody forms and call the boys' parents, he could not restrain a bit of "Golden Rule" moralizing. Turning to the older boy, he said, "How'd you like somebody to steal *your* stuff?" The boy became indignant and pouted back, "Ain't nobody gonna steal my stuff! I steals all my *own* stuff!" The officer was speechless.

Is such unabashed self-interest and exploitation a "natural" condition that can be altered only through proper moral and social training? Does it reflect a radically different subcultural conception of private property and reciprocity? Does it reflect an individually neglectful home? Or is it an unflattering comment on upward social mobility in a competitive society, a microcosm of social reality?

As a society, we really have no adequate answers to these questions. Our cultural heritage is strongly oriented toward the individual and his free will. Our country was founded largely on the principle of self-determination (in the common interest, however that is achieved). Yet we have reached the point where geographical frontiers are no longer available to absorb all those whose self-determination runs counter to accepted modes of achievement and competition. It is the prison and the reform school that do much of our absorbing now, and even the society at large has had to incorporate substantial controls into the economic structure to avoid an orgy of self-interest and exploitation.

We are indeed conflicted on the issue of individual culpability for criminal behavior, but our inaction leaves the police, the courts, and the prisons no choice. Most police officers, while recognizing the strong correlation between criminal behavior and bad environments, opt for a punishment-centered view of dealing with such behavior. It is admittedly a simplified way of viewing the situation, but it helps the police deal with the hostile feelings they develop toward hard-core criminals and delinquents and provides them with a rationale to justify the use of force when it becomes necessary.

When the officer walked by the four youths seated on a stoop one summer evening, their normal chatter ceased and they eyed him up and down. He ignored their show of scorn until he heard the wad of spit hit the sidewalk just behind his boots. Almost without thinking, he spun around and pointed his nightstick at the teenagers. "Get the fuck off those stairs and get moving!" he barked. The boys slowly walked away in their most expressive gaits, aware that their arrest could be imminent. No one spits that close to a policeman (unless he is new in the neighborhood and being tested), although black males often seem to use spitting from a distance as a gesture of defiance and contempt.

Contemplation of the spitting gesture (as an expression of animosity, its possible origin in the unsatisfied oral needs of

ghetto infants, and its symbolic place in the political conscious-
ness of an oppressed people) is a luxury for the police officer.
He usually does not have time to put things in a great deal of
perspective before he acts, although he always operates within
a certain practical perspective of his own. In the above case, he
passed four punks whose hatred of him was obvious and who
exceeded the accepted limits for the expression of that hatred.
He had to respond, or risk perhaps even greater abuse the next
time around.

Middle-class America's failure to accept on any but a
fantasy level the crude realities of violent human interactions ir-
ritates the police officer and causes him to feel that "intellec-
tuals," "liberals," and "do-gooders" are naive and overprotected.
And the fact that he is doing much of the overprotecting irks
the officer even further.

An officer went to a great deal of trouble one night to sub-
due a violent drunk who had injured his forehead in a fight.
With the prisoner finally handcuffed, the officer brought the
drunk to the emergency room of a city hospital where he was
met by a young intern. The doctor looked at the handcuffs on
the drunk, now quiet, and commanded the officer to remove
them. The officer protested, explaining that the drunk was unpredictable and could easily become violent again. The doctor
would have none of it and ordered the officer once again to
remove the handcuffs. "OK, Doc," he said, and unlocked the
cuffs. The drunk then lunged at the doctor and began beating
him. The officer waited for the doctor to ask that the cuffs be
placed back on the man. The doctor did so, quickly, and the
officer restrained the drunk with a double satisfaction.

After only a few months on the job, a police officer finds
himself reacting to drunks, doctors, and others in new ways.
The police culture and the perspective of policing change the
way an officer acts in a variety of situations. Police and house-
wives have something in common: they represent two of the
most underpaid and underappreciated generalist groups in the
country. And not many people take the generalist activities of
these groups seriously. When the housewife in the TV commer-
cial says that she is a cook, chauffeur, mother, lover, teacher,
maid, and hostess, we go along with the exaggeration because

we do not want to knock such an underappreciated group. Similarly, when someone makes a corny speech praising police officers as lawyers, marriage counsellors, ambulance drivers, diplomats, social workers, crime fighters, and obstetricians all rolled into one, no one takes this patronizing too seriously. Police *are* generalists, but generalists do not represent an aggregate of multiple specialties.

The general function of police is to create and maintain the order that is consistent with the principles of a political democracy. Police must have some skills in a wide variety of areas in order to do this job, and fighting crime is just one of several areas in which they become fairly proficient. In any event, police respond not so much to illegality as to disorder, which is why "disorderly conduct" is one of the most frequently used (and abused) categories of arrest. Anything unusual, loud, boisterous, or violent, anything alarming or unexpected catches an officer's attention, and the illegality of the activity is only one factor that goes into his decision to intervene or to ignore.[6] This "intervention reflex" in unusual situations gradually becomes part of an officer's way of behaving twenty-four hours a day. He gets used to asking people what they are doing in a certain area at a certain time. He gets used to following suspicious-looking cars (if only with his eyes) and to "eyeing" young males whose postures and expressions indicate a potentially hostile attitude toward others. He does not hesitate to give advice to parents about raising their children, to alcoholics who have not yet hit the skids, to teenagers who appear salvageable, or to citizens with legal problems. And the public expects him to do this. It may or may not be his idea of police work, but the role is there and he must fill it as he sees fit. He is a generalist in the field of public and even private *order,* whether he likes it or not.

When a new recruit arrives at the police academy, he probably envisions police work as primarily crime-oriented. This is most true for detectives, whose case-centered work and civilian clothes do not mark them as generalists. But the uniformed patrol officer will often describe his work as "85 percent horseshit," meaning that most of the work he does has nothing to do with any real crime.[7] It will involve people who have been bitten by dogs, people whose children have run away from home, old folks who have no one to talk to, and people whose ultimate response in any frustrating situation is to "call the cops."

It is true, particularly in poorer neighborhoods, that police provide medical and legal services normally performed by professional specialists in more affluent neighborhoods. They also provide an impromptu referral service to social agencies and hospitals.[8] But it is not accurate to describe police as obstetricians and lawyers. These activities by policemen, demanding though they be, are simply part of the general order-maintenance function of police. A police officer can do almost anything and truthfully say that it is just part of the job.

This all-inclusive order-maintenance role that police find themselves in is a source of both great satisfaction and tremendous frustration. There is a lot of variety in the work, and the officer is never sure of what he will have to deal with in any given tour of duty. Most officers who enjoy their work enjoy this variety and unpredictability. On the other hand, two attitudes join to take some of the fun out of the unpredictability of policing. The first is the officer's attitude, which sees his job as mainly crime-oriented and sees "routine calls for service" as so much garbage he has to put up with while awaiting the opportunity for a good pursuit and arrest.

The second attitude is the public view that the police should intervene in every situation that smacks remotely of conflict, even those that involve only petty neighbor-to-neighbor conflicts. Someone will call the police because his neighbor has raked leaves onto his property. A customer may call the police if he is not satisfied with his purchase and can get no satisfaction from the seller. A bartender will call the police to eject a drunk who should never have been given so many drinks in the first place. Cab drivers will call the police over a fare dispute. Yet most people, who are usually only casually acquainted with substantive law, do not realize that in many cases the police can do nothing to help but can only "lend an ear" for a few moments. And citizens' reactions to the reply that police can do nothing is often anger and suspicion that the officer is just dodging his duties. Of course, it also happens that people know full well that no police action is possible, but they will summon the police to the scene anyway, hoping that the arrival of authority will intimidate their particular antagonist into submission. The officer's knowledge that he is being used in this way is highly irritating, but he generally does not show his feelings too overtly. Not only is he a bit afraid of citizen complaints to his superiors, but also he is accustomed to a certain amount of public ignorance in the areas of law and legal responsibility.

CHAPTER 3

Police Discretion

ONE OF THE reasons that the "crime-fighter" image of police persists so strongly is an administrative one. If police respond only to outright violations of the law, and if they respond to *all* such violations (as their oath of office states they will), there are only limited problems of accountability. Was too much force used in the arrest? Was the right man arrested? Were there legal grounds for arrest? Were proper procedures followed in processing the arrested individual? But if police administrators ever admitted openly that their officers use a great deal of discretion in enforcing the law or in using their authority to maintain order, they would be putting themselves in the nightmarish predicament of accounting for every act or failure to act by a police officer. Admitting the substantial use of discretion by officers would open the door to charges that police are arbitrary in their dealings with the public, that their performance varies with their moods, or that certain police decisions are motivated by prejudice or favor.[1]

Police discretion is in much the same position as the issue of "quotas." Everyone knows they exist, but police administrators must deny that they exist in order to protect the image of police as solely crime fighters. The fear of these administrators that the public will take them to task over these issues is no doubt well founded. But the failure of administrators and citizenry alike to come to terms with reality is a serious obstacle to improved police service and police-citizen communication. The reality of police discretion, being so well camouflaged and denied, is not well understood.

At bottom, police discretion involves a decision on the officer's part to intervene or not to intervene. That decision is the result of a complex of factors about which the officer makes judgments prior to his exercise of discretion. The first factor (but not necessarily the most important) is his own perception of his role in the situation. Is it any of his business to intervene? Is it a "police matter" as he interprets it?

One evening an officer was walking his beat past a group of run-down rowhouses when he heard a man shouting and cursing, and some muffled barks of a dog. The commotion was inside a house and probably involved a man beating his dog. After a little hesitation, the officer knocked loudly on the door. A man about thirty years old, who was known around the neighborhood as a "mental case," answered. He was breathing heavily and frothing at the corners of his mouth. "What's going on in there?" the officer demanded. "Nothing," answered the man. "Bullshit, pal. I heard you hollerin' and screamin' in there. Now what's going on? Are you beating that dog?" "No, sir, I'm not." "Bullshit. Let me tell you something. If I hear you laying into that dog again, I'm going to take you in for cruelty to animals, you hear?" "Yes, sir," was the frightened answer.

The officer learned later that the dog had chewed up a portion of the man's mattress and was being punished for misbehaving. Now that in itself is not really a police matter. But in this case the officer decided that the frenzied quality of the man's screaming constituted a basis for intervention. He interpreted the situation as one demanding his attention as the maintainer of order in the neighborhood. Other factors went into his decision, too, his fondness for animals, for instance, and the possibility of a "cruelty to animals" crime. In addition, there was nothing more important occupying him at the time. As we shall see, most discretionary decisions are based on multiple factors. But the principal factor in this case was the officer's perception of his role as order-maintainer. He reacted to a violent-sounding situation because that is what he thought he was supposed to do as a policeman.

A second factor involved in discretionary decision-making is the citizen's perception of the police role. When the rookie officer first walks or drives his beat, he often forgets that a long history of police-citizen interactions precedes him. He is heir to a set of mutual expectations and assumptions about his role that he may not even be aware of.

It was the rookie's first week walking his beat in a ghetto neighborhood. He rounded the corner and approached a bar about sixty yards down the street. In front of the bar was a group of about five or six men engaged in some casual corner-hanging and conversation. When they saw the officer approaching, they fell silent and disbanded, some going inside the bar and some walking off down the street. The rookie was amazed at his power but could not understand what had happened. Had the group stayed on the corner, he would have walked right by and not said a word. In days to come, he learned that it was expected that he "run 'em off the corners" in front of bars and liquor stores. It was against a city ordinance to loiter in front of bars. In this case, the expectations of the men that the officer was going to "run 'em" did his work for him.

Sometimes an officer is obliged to make decisions that conflict with his own preferences in order to carry on the tradition of order-maintenance characteristic of the area he is patrolling.

When the officer looked down the alley between two streets of decaying rowhouses, he saw a familiar enough sight about thirty yards away—four men passing a bottle of cheap wine. Were he to respond strictly to the dictates of law, he would have arrested all four for "drinking on a public street." But he could not be bothered. What were they doing—ruining the image of the neighborhood? He looked around at the filth and laughed at the idea. He would have preferred to leave them alone, but he could not. They expected him to intervene, so intervene he must or risk getting the reputation of cowardice or softness. He approached the by now highly nervous men and asked for the bottle. In their ignorance of the law, they had placed it on the ground, thinking that the physical separation would make their arrest impossible. The officer retrieved the bottle and four sets of horror-struck eyes watched as the contents splashed onto the alley. "You should go to jail," he said to no one in particular. "Now get moving."

In a middle-class neighborhood the officer is not expected to intervene as often as he does in a poorer neighborhood. People see him more as a public servant than as "the Man." He is expected to overlook minor parking violations and crowds in front of bars (unless the crowd is teenage). People do not drink in alleys because they have enough money to buy a drink at the bar, and they do not spill over into the streets as easily as poorer people, for whom the "public" street is often an extension of their own limited private property. There are fewer opportunities for police intervention in a middle-class neighborhood, and thus less of a history that the officer must live up to. The major cause of his interventions in these neighborhoods is teenagers, both delinquent and non-delinquent. And the mobility of these adolescents means that the "car stop" is going to be one of an officer's major discretionary decisions. Any "souped-up" car is fair game here. A raised rear end, a loud muffler, a squealing acceleration, a large number of passengers, or any of the countless safety equipment violations (taillights, taglights, insufficient tread on tires, dashboard lights, etc., etc.) justify a car stop that often leads to an alcohol or narcotics arrest, a stolen car, or a person wanted on a warrant.

When the two officers pulled over the red Plymouth with its taglight out, they envisioned a quick issuance of a "safety repair order" and the resumption of their patrol. The one officer hoped so, because his partner's zeal for issuing safety repair orders was irritating. Let's face it, you can stop almost any car on the road and find something wrong with it. So he had stayed in the cruiser while his partner approached the driver of the stopped car. But soon his partner was motioning for him to approach the passenger side of the vehicle, and he sprung out of the cruiser, aware that car stops can on occasion be extremely unpredictable and hazardous. As it turned out, there were three bottles of beer on the front seat (opened) and the passenger was only seventeen. The officer who had approached the passenger side recalled his own youth and favored pouring out the beer and leaving well enough alone. The seventeen-year-old was scared and seemed like a nice kid. But it was his partner's show, and he deferred to his decision to arrest the boy and the driver of the car, a twenty-one-year-old man. The two youths were taken to the station and charged with alcohol violations. The seventeen-year-old was charged with possession, and the twenty-one-year-old was charged with furnishing alcohol to a minor. The arresting officer had decided not to charge the older youth with driving-while-intoxicated because that would have entailed a trip downtown to the "breathalyzer" and to traffic court. Also, since it was near quitting time, it would have entailed substantial overtime which the officer did not want that night. In addition, there was doubt as to whether the driver had consumed enough beer to warrant a "drunk driving" charge.

There were many factors involved in the decision to arrest and the decisions as to which charges to prefer, but the primary factor in the decision to arrest was the personality of the arresting officer. Now, the arresting officer would be the first to deny that his personality entered into the arrest. He would state that he observed a violation of the law and responded as his oath of office dictates. And you cannot prove him wrong. If an officer interprets his job in a strictly legalistic way, denying any arbitrariness in the exercise of his discretion, then theoretically his personality is irrelevant to the job. However, the facts are otherwise. This officer exercised his discretion in a variety of situations and frankly enjoyed the potential for manipulation and enforcement that he possessed. What we revere as "the law" is, after all, only an imperfect tool for establishing and maintaining orderly relations among citizens. The officer uses this tool as he sees fit, within certain administrative and judicial guidelines.[2] "The law" is, in fact, an agent of the police officer, not vice-versa.

What is the "personality" of the police officer? Psychologists have been trying for years to define personality, but they have not yet succeeded to everyone's satisfaction. "Personality" as a unitary concept probably has only limited utility. But it can be broken down into categories that are a little more manageable. One of these categories is *temperament*. Some officers are more quick-tempered and excitable than others. Some are always calm and deliberate, refusing to get too worked up over the routines of their work. Another category might loosely be called *attitudes*. Some officers are more kindly disposed toward certain racial, ethnic, sexual, or generational groups than others. And while most officers are generally conservative in their morals and politics, some are less conservative than others about such things as public demonstrations, marijuana use, pornography, and black politicians.

A third, and most important, category of personality is the *dynamics* of the individual. Did an officer become what he is out of some adolescent desire to wear a gun and drive a patrol car? Does an officer frankly enjoy exercising power and authority over others at his whim? Is he carrying a chip on his shoulder? Does he find the possibility of witnessing, or even participating in, bloody and violent encounters deeply fascinating? Some more positive dynamics might involve a desire to establish order and peace in one's environment, a desire to take control of situations which are beyond the control of others (e.g., marital disputes), a need to "do something" concrete to counteract antisocial behavior, or a need to be different—to stand out in some way in the community as a person with courage and responsibility.

A fourth category of personality might be called *traits*. These would simply be qualities characteristic of the person, and there is really no limit on how many traits we can attribute to an individual. It all depends on how completely we wish to describe him. Some of the more important traits in a police officer are self-control, punitiveness, open- or narrow-mindedness, alertness, suspiciousness, patience, and endurance (emotional as well as physical, though the two interact).

An officer who is narrow-minded and punitive, and who takes everything as a personal affront to his authority, is a dangerous individual on the street, regardless of his dynamics or attitudes. This danger is heightened if the officer has poor self-control. And the danger applies to other policemen as well as to the public.

In every district there will be a small handful of officers who have a poor sense of humor, whose temper and "touchiness" isolate them and leave them largely friendless, and whose attitude toward their job is one of dead seriousness. These officers see themselves as strict enforcers of the law and would deny that they are almost wholly identified with their function as police. They generally make a lot of arrests—often for "disorderly conduct—issue a lot of traffic tickets, and find themselves in court more than other officers. Their colleagues see them as "gung-ho" and ridicule their "statistics" as mostly provoked and "chickenshit," the sort of thing anyone could do were he willing to aggravate the citizenry in the name of law enforcement.

These officers are, I believe, unfit for their work because they lack flexibility, perspective, and the capacity for sympathy. They are to a large extent as anti-social as the "criminals" they arrest. They survive in police work mainly because we insist on defining policing as a down-the-line enforcement function. They give discretion a bad name because they are, by nature, incapable of distinguishing arbitrariness from sound judgment. They are dangerous to their craft and to those who practice it by their sides.

Most officers do not fit this bill. Their traits are generally more positive. They are active and restless. They seek more than the usual amount of variety and excitement in their work —"stimulus hunger," one author calls it.[3] They keep cooler than most of us would in tight situations. They have a well-honed and brutally honest sense of humor, in spite of (or perhaps because of) their constant exposure to human weakness and cruelty. They are suspicious but not paranoically so given the demands of their job. They are never as alert as their academy instructors warned them to be, for as Macluhan once wrote, "The price of eternal vigilance is indifference," and they would rather be relaxed than indifferent.

The key thing to remember in this discussion of "police personality" is that police are *ordinary men in extraordinary circumstances*. There is nothing terribly unusual about police officers as a group that would distinguish them from "the public" as a group.[4] The traits, attitudes, temperaments, and dynamics described above are mentioned, not because police have a monopoly on them, but because the circumstances of their work make them particularly relevant to the exercise of enforcement discretion. A bartender who does not like blacks can water down the drinks he serves to black people. A waitress can be gruff and rude. A professional person can be condescending or obtuse. And anyone can manifest his likes and dislikes for others in countless ways. This is all the exercise of discretion. But only in rare cases (commitment to mental hospitals, for example) are the consequences of the exercise of work-related discretion so critical or personally important as in police work. A black man can live with a watered-down drink, or he can go to another bar, or he can sue the place or refuse to leave a tip. But he cannot wipe out an arrest record or a jail term. And there is little he can do to harm the police officer who caused all this, provided that the officer was polite and did not abuse the man in any way.

Perhaps the main reason a discussion of the police personality is important is not so much that personality influences decisions (which is true, and intuitively sensed by us all), but that many people hold rather stereotypical and negative ideas about the police. Given (or sometimes not given) rough demographic data about the educational and socio-economic levels of police, their usually conservative political leanings, and their quasi-military organization, people often assume that authoritarian or even sadistic tendencies dominate "police personalities." Yet more detailed studies usually portray a different picture. One study, using various objective and projective personality tests as well as an intelligence test, found that officers had high intelligence (average score, 113) and "superior personality adjustment."[5] Robert Hogan interpreted the results of this study in light of findings from additional research[6] and concluded that the average police officer:

1) prefers action to contemplation;
2) is masculine in his style and manner of behavior;
3) is natural, free from pretense, and unaffected;
4) has a narrow range of interests;
5) gets along well in the world as it is, is socially appropriate in his behavior, and keeps out of trouble.[7]

Hogan also studied the characteristics of Maryland State Police cadets and probationary officers who were evaluated by their supervisors along a dimension of "overall suitability for police work." These ratings were correlated with an empathy scale[8] and with the eighteen standard scales of the California Psychological Inventory to discover the qualities of effective, rather than just average, police officers. Hogan's conclusions are as follows:

> Examining these scales individually, highly rated Maryland police compared with men in general are forceful and self-confident (Dominance); they are affiliative and outgoing (Sociability); self-confident and sure of themselves (Self-acceptance). These men also have a sense of energy and good health (Well-being); they endorse the rules and values of the society (Responsibility Achievement via Conformance). In the correlation with Well-being Responsibility, and Achievement via Conformance, there is an expected emphasis on conformity, conservatism, and rule-following. Finally, the effective policeman is characterized by a competitive spirit (Achievement via Conformity and Achievement via Independence), and particularly by functional intelligence (Intellectual Efficiency). . . .
>
> Finally, the popular image of the policeman as an authoritarian personality is simply not true for the effective police officers in this example. The Tolerance scale of the California Psychological Inventory was empirically keyed against the California F scale . . . a measure of intolerance and potential anti-democratic, or fascist, tendencies. Thus, the Tolerance scale is a subtle, inverse measure of intolerance and authoritarian tendencies. The average correlation of .18 between police effectiveness and Tolerance suggests that the good policeman is somewhat more, rather than less, tolerant and democratic than the average man.[9]

There is another aspect of personality we will briefly discuss—the issue of inherent vs. acquired traits. Rokeach,[10] for instance, cites a number of studies showing police to be cynical, suspicious, isolated from personal friends and from the public, suffering from feelings of powerlessness and self-hate, preoccupied with obtaining "respect for the law," unquestionably accepting of orders, politically conservative, and about as dogmatic and authoritarian as the populations from which they are drawn. However, there is no mention of whether these qualities are present in men who, because of them, seek out a police career, or whether the occupational demands of policing change men in certain ways to make them "different" from the rest of us. Rokeach himself is fairly conscientious on this score. For instance, when police were matched with a comparable non-police sample, only eight out of thirty-six values (Rokeach's own test of values) stood out as significantly distinguishing police from non-police. This suggests that some value changes observed in police may well be due to occupational demands rather than the more "internal-oriented" processes of individual dynamics (though a certain interaction of the two is obviously going to occur). But by the same token, "our data suggest that (within the less educated groups from which police are traditionally recruited) recruitment is more likely to take place from among those who place a relatively lower value on "freedom," "equality," "independence," and "a world of beauty" and from among those who place a relatively higher value on "obedience," "self-control," "a comfortable life," and "pleasure."[11] This suggests that certain people seem "cut out" for police work, as that work is presently defined, and differ from their fellows even before the situational demands of policing have worked their effects on personality.

Although Rokeach's descriptions are necessarily limited by his measures, the distinction he makes between "differential recruitment" and "socialization" in studying the origin of police personality attributes is an important one to make. Many critics of police have written them off as innately gruff, brutal, or crude with no thought as to whether police *are* that way or are sometimes made to appear that way by a job which, after all, they and all of us help to define.

The influence of an officer's personality on the decisions he makes cannot be ignored, denied, or wished away. This influence is operative every day and will continue to be. Even if an officer's decisions were always fair (whether or not they were impartial), this would be the result of his ability for self-control, perspective, and empathy—aspects of his personality. Even the strictly legalistic officer operates from a certain personality point of view. What we need to do, then, is select those aspects of personality that seem most conducive to the exercise of sound police discretion. We need to screen out pathological dynamics and unstable temperaments. Attitudes are none of our business, provided that traits of self-control and self-knowledge are strong. The officer's and the public's best means of insuring mature discretionary decisions is a reasonably thorough understanding by the officer of his own dynamics, traits, and attitudes. If he knows, for example, that marital disputes cause him to tense up, become angry, and side with the wife, he can counteract for this tendency by realizing what is going on inside himself. Exploring his own history with regard to parental squabbles, or with regard to his own marriage, might help him develop some perspective on his handling of such disputes.

A different sort of factor in police discretion is the administrative one. To illustrate:

It was 11:15 at night, and the footman had less than forty-five minutes to go before he could get home for some sleep. A small crowd had gathered on a corner in front of a bar where a man and a woman were arguing loudly. The officer approached and stood on the corner for a few seconds, hoping that his mere presence would provide a strong hint for the people to move back inside the bar. It did not, and the man, drunk and seemingly mentally unstable to boot, continued shouting and cursing. He removed his jacket and threw it on the ground to emphasize a point he was making about the woman's character. Strictly speaking, at this point the man could have been arrested for disorderly conduct. The officer walked up to the man and told him to get back in the bar or move on, but not to stay on the corner. The man, breathing heavily and looking quite crazed to the officer, replied, "Naw, I ain't movin'! I'm upset!" The officer who, once again strictly speaking, now had double grounds for arrest—disorderly conduct and loitering—answered, "Look, man, I know you're upset but you've gotta move off the corner, OK?" The officer placed his hand in a friendly manner on the man's shoulder as if to guide him along. But the man held his ground and hissed, "Get your hands offa me!" At this point, only the late hour and his reluctance to go to court early the next morning kept the officer from arresting the man. "Lock

him up," pouted the woman with whom the man had been
fighting. The officer reached for the microphone to his radio
and, holding it up as if to speak, said to the man, "Look, pal,
I'm going to call the wagon if you don't get movin', understand?
You want me to call the wagon?" "Lock him up!" repeated the
woman. "I don't want to lock him up if I don't have to," the
officer barked back at her. He was irritated by the woman's attempt to use him and by the fact that in any street encounter a
woman has incredible advantages over a man. After all, she
may have started the whole business, regardless of who was
being the loudest at the present time. A few seconds later, the
man and his coterie of onlookers walked away. (Two days later
he threatened a gas station owner with a knife and escaped on
foot.)

    The officer had found the man's rebuffs infuriating, but he
nevertheless nursed the situation to a peaceful finish, not only
because of a desire to see things end peacefully, but also because
any arrests made that late in the shift would have necessitated
unwanted overtime plus getting up early the next morning for
court. If an out-and-out crime had been committed, the officer
would have made the arrest with no hesitation. But this situation, as are most, was a "judgment call" in which arrest was
the last resort.

    If the officer had been receiving a lot of pressure from his
sergeant to "get his arrest stats up," he might have decided differently. If the man had spit at or struck the officer, his response would have been reflexively punitive, and appropriately
so. Such gross insults to an officer's right to do his job are the
only situations outside of felonies-in-progress that bring an immediate and predictable response from police. But most of their
decisions are not made without some more or less careful review of administrative and other factors.

    Another administrative factor is as follows: Would anyone
around complain to my superiors if I were to handle this situation as I want to handle it? The role of crime fighter can be
held over an officer's head, and every time he makes a decision
not to arrest where an arrest could, legalistically, be made, he
takes a chance that someone will complain about his alleged
inaction. The see-a-crime-arrest-the-criminal reflex is one of the

fictions of police work which lends itself to misinterpretation by those who think that an officer is as overjoyed as they are at the possibility of wreaking vengeance on wrongdoers' heads.

It was 11:40 at night—less than twenty minutes to go before shift change. The officer received a call for a group of teenagers drinking on a corner in a residential neighborhood. Seconds later he pulled up to the corner, got out of his car, and approached the boys. By this time, of course, all the beer was sitting in the gutter so that each boy could repeat the litany of innocence: "It's not mine, I don't know whose it is." The officer picked up the beer, poured it out, and ordered the boys off the corner. "But I live right here," protested one. "I don't care where you live," was the reply. "I got a complaint" worked wonders and the boys moved on, speculating on which old lady in the neighborhood turned them in. As the officer radioed in "Complaint abated" to the dispatcher and noted the complaint number of the call on his log sheet, he looked up at the windows around the corner, just a bit worried that someone would be disappointed that six specimens of degenerate youth had not been arrested.

Still another factor in discretionary decisions is the degree of illegality or amount of disorder present in the situation. An officer who wants to keep his job wastes no time in intervening in assault, rape, homicide, robbery, burglary, and auto theft calls. In general, wherever there is a serious threat to life or property, police will not hesitate to respond, regardless of administrative, personality, or other factors. After all, this is what many of them joined the police department for, and such action is the stuff on which they feed. But an individual officer may go several days, weeks, or even months without personally encountering one of these serious calls. In the meantime, his hours are filled with calls that involve considerable interpretation on his part as to the degree of disorder involved. Some such calls are "disorderly juveniles" (usually playing ball loudly), "disorderly person," "suspicious person," "loud party," "marriage dispute," "verbal assault" or "assault by threat," "automobiles racing," and "intoxicated person." Although there is the constant danger that one of these "minor" calls may erupt into something major, most of them can be handled short of arrest, even when, strictly speaking, some minor violation of the law may have occurred.

Many students of police discretion (usually with a background in law and judicial processes) often focus on the arrest process itself, or its failure to be employed where it could be, as the core of enforcement discretion. Thus Joseph Goldstein maintains in a well-circulated sentence, "Police decisions not to invoke the criminal process determine the outer limits of law enforcement."[12] There seems to be a rough consensus among these scholars that the arrest process, being a serious one, should not be left to the unexamined discretion of individual officers. They point out the great need for specific departmental policy decisions that could be made explicit to police and citizens alike, regardless of the dictates of legislated policies (laws). Thus a police chief could announce (and make explicit) what is currently clouded in a fog of citizen resentment and seemingly (as well as real) arbitrary enforcement. He could, for example, announce that during rush hours no speeding tickets will be issued on main arteries for speeds less than ten miles over the posted limit. There are interesting and urgently needed steps to be taken in such directions, but considerable obstacles would have to be overcome, not the least of which would be the removal of the legalistic defense police administrators use to mask the complex (and only indirectly controlled) decisions of their subordinates. However, legal scholars often assume (perhaps because of their specialized focus on judicial procedures) that when an officer decides not to arrest, he therefore has done nothing at all in response to the situation in question. This is simply not true, although it is by no means uncommon for officers to ignore some situations. As Bittner points out, the decision not to make an arrest is rarely, if ever, merely a decision not to act; it is most often a decision to act alternatively.[13] When an officer does not arrest in situations where he could arrest, he may have given a verbal warning, a reprimand, or a threat of future arrest. Or he may have negotiated a settlement of some sort. Or he may have "defused" a situation, as when he pours wine out in an alley, takes a pocket knife from a juvenile, disperses a crowd, calms an insistent complainant, or "gives a lecture" of some kind. Even "giving someone a break" can have a powerful deterrent effect. Officers can usually tell which persons can benefit from leniency and which will take it only as a sign of weakness (grateful though they be for it). By being "easy" and forgiving toward an anxious and upset "violator," the officer can, through his decision not to arrest, provide a flood of relief and can elicit a determined resolution to avoid the improper behavior in the future. I have occasionally been thankful that most police officers are temperamentally direct and forthright. For if an officer were so inclined, he could engage in endless alienating manipulations with the public, using his office and the tradition of police right to invade personal space in public settings to "play with" people for his own peculiar enjoyment.

On every call, the officer must evaluate whether any police action is necessary, whether it is possible (the "suspicious person" may have fled, or the complainant may not have revealed his identity to the police), and whether the complaint is of a sufficiently minor nature that he can dispense with writing a report and give the dispatcher one of six "oral codes" to indicate the nature of his decision and the outcome of the call (A = complaint unfounded; B = unable to locate complainant; C = no such address; D = no police action necessary; E = suspects gone by time police arrive; F = complaint abated).

On a busy night, some incidents that could be written up on an "MI" report (miscellaneous incident) will be coded by the officer so that he can return to service quickly and handle the backlog of calls. A case of "telephone misuse" (threatening or obscene calls), for example, really should go on an "MI." But an officer on a busy night might code it "D" over the air and advise the complainant to contact the telephone company, who will handle the matter in the long run anyway or at least until the caller is identified. If the phone company wants to see a police report, they can get it on a less busy night.

Another factor—and a touchy one indeed—involves the attitude and demeanor of the person whose legal fate it is that the officer is deciding. Let us take the following example:

Two officers on foot patrol rounded the corner into a trash-strewn alley and surprised three men drinking a bottle of wine. One officer anticipated a pour-it-out-and-get-moving routine, but the other officer had different ideas. He smiled at the nervous men and said, "Now what do you want to go drinking in the alley for?" Two of the men grinned and mumbled, unsure of the game that was about to be played. The third man remained silent and expressionless. The officer turned to this man and said, still smiling, "Where do you live?" "Over on the West side," was the sullen answer. "No—I mean what's your address?" The officer's smile was disappearing. "The 400 block of Frank Street," hedged the man defiantly. The officer was no longer smiling. He had wanted an exact address. "I want to know exactly where you live," he said. "What for?" answered the man. At that point the officer placed him under arrest, searched him, and called for the wagon to transport the man to jail. One of the man's partners quickly left the scene, but the other stayed to urge the officer to go easy on his friend. The officer then placed *him* under arrest for interfering with an arrest. (Later, at the jail, the desk sergeant pointed out the transparency of this charge, and so the man was charged with disorderly conduct instead.) The first man was charged with drinking on a public street (he had been holding the bottle at the time), and the two were carted off to jail.

This example contains most of the elements needed for a discussion of police response to citizens' "attitude problems." To begin with, there is no clear-cut right or wrong in the incident just described. The men *were* breaking the law in drinking on a public street, even though their behavior in that neighborhood at that time was certainly no cause for anything more than a "chickenshit" arrest, if that. The officers had to intervene because of the mutual expectations of all concerned. But while one officer considered the men's attitudes toward the police irrelevant to that particular situation and would have dealt merely with the overt act by pouring out the wine or telling the men to move inside, the other officer (who had seniority) decided to play with the men. This officer generally took every interaction on the street personally and enjoyed toying with people's anxieties prior to making his decisions. This was the reason for his smiling at the men in the alley, and for asking them irrelevant questions.[14] But he ran into problems. One of the men resented being played with in this fashion. (The fact that he was on probation from a five-year prison sentence may have had some bearing on his stony attitude.) The officer pushed for information, the man hedged, and was arrested as much for his defiant attitude as for drinking in public. The arrest of the second man was an act of pure whimsy on the officer's part, for at that point the wine had all but been forgotten save as legalistic grounds for the first man's arrest.

In this case the officer might justifiably be accused of misusing his authority, although he could always hide behind the half-truth that he was only responding to an outright violation of the law. On the other hand, the attitudes of citizens *are* often important clues as to their future behavior. If a person caught in some violation of the law seems genuinely regretful, an officer might infer that the person made a mistake and will try not to do it again. (Contrary to popular belief, excessive obsequiousness and shows of deference only irritate many officers.) If, however, the person is hostile, abusive, and defiant, the officer can only infer that he has no intention of altering his behavior and will repeat his violation on other occasions. Such a person cannot be "let off the hook" but must suffer some negative consequences in order to "teach him a lesson."[15]

In our example, the man in the alley was defiant but did not bristle with more than the usual hostility young black males so often have for the police. His defiance sprang from resentment of the officer's game-playing and not from any private resolution to spend the rest of his days drinking in alleys (in which case he could not be taught any lessons anyway). The officer's tendency to interpret *all* interactions solely in terms of his personal authority blinded him to the meaning of the man's attitude and to the workings of his own narrow dynamics. In any event, it is futile to believe that ghetto men who consistently drink wine in alleys will ever cease to do so as long as there are ghettoes, men, and alleys. The most appropriate police response is simply to deal with behaviors (arrest the men or pour out the wine) and ignore attitudes that cannot be changed.

Police officers who wish to avoid ulcers and migraines sooner or later learn to tolerate considerable verbal and nonverbal abuse from citizens. At first an officer will tend to compartmentalize the public so that working a black neighborhood is "bad" and working a white neighborhood is "good." Teenagers cannot be trusted, but old folks and children are friendly. He will do this on the basis of his perception of how they feel toward him. He will be greeted more often and smiled at in a white neighborhood and will feel more at home there. The converse of all this may or may not be true for a black officer.[16]

It was the rookie's second month walking a ghetto beat. As he walked down the sidewalk, he noticed an old black man standing on a porch smoking a pipe. The man was across the street, so the officer smiled congenially and waved to the nice old man. The man removed his pipe from his mouth, savored some expectoration for a moment, and spat a silent "Fuck off" onto the sidewalk below.

After enough exposure to all sorts of people in all sorts of neighborhoods, the officer will back off from his earlier generalizations (though he never abandons them completely) and will take each person on his own merits. This is the ideal. An alternate, and frequent, outcome is a generalized mistrust of and hostility toward *all* citizens, so that "the public" as a whole becomes a dangerous and alien mass, punctuated by isolated instances of warmth and respect toward the officer. Aggravating this situation is the strong tendency on the part of many people to use and manipulate police to their own advantage in personal affairs. At any rate, the long-term reaction of officers to years of dealing with "the public" is a strong skepticism that slowly becomes a pervasive cynicism about the human condition.[17]

An officer answered a call for a "disorderly subject in a house" and was "backed up" by three other units because the address was that of a convicted murderer out on probation after serving two years of his sentence. The officers were met in front of the house by a woman who stated that she had taken out a warrant for the arrest of the man upstairs (the man on probation) because he had beaten her the previous night. The man leaned out the upstairs window and shouted at the woman, "What'd you call the police for? Can't you talk to me without the police?" The officers demanded that he come out, but he refused. They then contacted the dispatcher to run a "warrant check" on the man. If the woman had indeed taken out a warrant for the man's arrest, they could break down the door and take the man. Knowing his prior record, the officers readied a shotgun and settled down for the 15-minute wait on the warrant check. In the meantime, the woman said she was going upstairs to pack her things and would be right down. When she entered the house, shouting began and then subsided. The officers waited on the sidewalk, keeping a watchful eye on the upstairs window for the appearance of a revolver or a rifle barrel. After several minutes had elapsed in which the officers had prepared themselves mentally for a potentially violent assault on the house, the woman emerged followed by the man. But she had not packed a thing. As the officers approached the man, the radio announced "No warrant on file," and the whole scene came to a crashing anticlimax. The man and the woman walked down the street arm-in-arm without a word to the police.

In this case the officers had readied themselves to risk their lives to take the man into custody on the basis of the woman's claim that she had taken out a warrant on him. At the very least, the police had facilitated some sort of reconciliation between the two. But they received no thanks whatsoever, not even the acknowledgement that they had prepared to risk their lives. They had literally been used, as they are used thousands of times every day by unsympathetic citizens preoccupied with immediate personal concerns.

A final factor to be considered in the exercise of discretion is one that will be dealt with in the next chapter—the pressure of one's peers. In police work the regard and respect of one's colleagues is vitally important. In order to earn and maintain this respect, he must occasionally choose a course of action that, among other things, meets with the approval of his fellow officers. He must not be "too soft," and while it is difficult to be considered "too hard" without bordering on outright brutality, he must confine his hardness to "hardened criminals." An officer who is excessively physical in his handling of juveniles, for example, will be suspected of cowardice or "bullyism."[18] If he is excessively tolerant, the word will spread that "they're carrying away his post," i.e., getting away with much more than "they" should. Not only is his own reputation at stake, but the work patterns of his colleagues are at stake too. If a too-lenient officer has a beat for a week, the officer who inherits that beat from him has to work extra hard to repair the damage done to the system of mutual expectations between citizens and police in that neighborhood.

CHAPTER 4

The Pressures
of Policing

You cannot see small police successes. You cannot see police failures. Even if you have been inside the station house—even if you have ridden in a squad car—there are countless things invisible to you, countless subtle pressures that act on police from day to day, year in and year out, to shape what they do and determine who they are.[1]

ONCE AGAIN, THE key phrase to remember in understanding the pressures involved in policing is "ordinary men in extraordinary circumstances."[2] Although police officers may be extraordinary enough as individuals, as a group they do not stand out in any unusual way from most of the population they police.[3] An elaborate application and screening procedure insures that those applicants who are accepted are indeed "average" by conventional standards. Intensive interviews and investigations into the personal life of the applicant, including his marital, criminal, occupational, educational, and sexual history, are conducted. Some large departments include an interview with a psychologist as part of the screening procedure, and even visit the applicant in his home to check on its cleanliness and order. Often the applicant's wife is interviewed to make sure she has no more than the usual wifely objections to her husband's career choice, and to see if she is aware of the strains her husband's desired job can cause in a marriage. In addition, most departments of any size now include a polygraph examination to verify an applicant's statements concerning such things as drug use, sexual habits, drinking habits, criminal record, and the like.

The net result of all this screening is a relatively conventional group of police recruits. They have never been in any serious trouble, they have normal sexual and drug-use histories, they have never participated in any civil rights or political demonstrations, they have never belonged to any political extremist organizations (right- or left-wing), and they verbalize conventionally conservative opinions on obscenity laws, due process, and enforcement of marijuana laws. They are of slightly higher than average intelligence and ambition, and generally subscribe to the standard American conception of "the good life," that is, home ownership, material comfort, higher education for their children, and the like. They are reasonably contented with their jobs, given their low expectations of the satisfactions to be derived from "a job," and they find meaning in their lives mostly within their own homes and families.[4]

These police recruits could just as well be firemen, mailmen, skilled laborers, or craftsmen. They identify for the most part with the mores and values of this middle-income group, and most recruits become policemen not out of any burning passion to police but from the simple belief that it is an economically secure job with a reasonable amount of variety and stimulation.[5]

Police departments make efforts to attract college graduates, but the heart and soul of almost every department remains basically "anti-intellectual" and scornful of "book learning." Certainly the police suspicion about participation in political demonstrations, the use of soft drugs, and the voicing of any but the more conventional moral attitudes rules out substantial numbers of young men and women who have graduated from college since the mid-1960s.[6]

When the college-graduate applicant showed up for his final interview before a three-man admissions board, he carried his diploma with him as he had been instructed. He was led into the room and shook hands with the three veteran police interviewers. They all sat down, and one of the interviewers asked to see the applicant's diploma. He looked it over and noticed that it was written in Latin. "You speak Latin?" he queried. "I can understand a little," replied the applicant. "Oh yeah?" said the interviewer. "Read this for me." The applicant took the diploma, believing in his naïveté that the interviewer was really interested. It was only when he finished translating part of the first sentence that he glanced up and caught the snickers being exchanged by the interviewers. Embarrassed, he pretended that he did not understand the rest of the Latin. The interview went on to other topics but did not improve in tone. He told the interviewers what they wanted to hear—simple, conservative opinions spoken with simplistic conviction—and the interview ended. As he left the room, he was reprimanded by the interviewer who had asked him to translate for not having the proper date of his graduation on the diploma. The applicant had been in infantry basic training in South Carolina on the day his class graduated, but he received the reprimand politely and was excused from the room. He was accepted for admission to the department.

So much for the nastier aspects of conventionalism. Times are changing, and in the next five to ten years, as the World War II crop of administrators retires or passes away, police departments will become more flexible and appreciative of non-technological innovations.

In the meantime, we must understand that police are not endowed with any extraordinary strength or sense of perspective to make the pressures we are about to discuss any more bearable. These pressures fall into three major categories: intradepartmental, extradepartmental, and inherent.[7] We have touched on some of these pressures already. There is, for instance, the pressure to produce evidence in the form of "statistics" that one is indeed "fighting crime." This is an intradepartmental pressure applied to the street officer by his sergeant, who is in turn pressured by the lieutenant, who is in turn pressured by the captain who is pressured by the major, etc., etc., etc., on up the administrative ladder. Where does this end? The commissioner or chief of police is answerable to city councils, mayors, legislators, and, in some instances, governors, who shape the

sort of policing they think you and I want. And that is where
it ends. In the long run (and it is, admittedly, a very long run
through much smoke-screening and distortion) it is the public
that is responsible for such things as "quotas" and meaningless
statistics accumulated by police departments.[8] You and I are
the ones who, ultimately, cast our police in the role of crime
fighters and thus hold them solely responsible for crime prevention. One of the more frustrating experiences for a police officer
is the issuance of summonses to appear in court to testify in
criminal cases. If, say, a person's stereo is stolen and the police
are lucky enough to apprehend the thief, the person is very
happy to get his stereo back and enjoys a moment of vengeance
as the handcuffed prisoner is carted off to jail. But two days
later, when the officer knocks on the person's door to give him
his summons to appear in court to testify against the thief, he
often shows only annoyance and resentment. In fact, he will
often go to great lengths to create the impression that he is not
at home and thus cannot receive the summons.

It was 2:30 in the morning. A man looked out the rear
window of his rowhouse to see two teenage boys removing
clothing from a neighbor's clothesline. He rushed to the phone
to call the police. But his initial impulse was squelched by a reluctance to "get involved," so he refused to give the emergency
call clerk at police headquarters any specific information lest
he be identified as a witness and have to take part in any court
proceedings. He told the clerk only that two boys were taking
clothes off a line on Langley Avenue (no block number). Refusing to give his name, he hung up. Not surprisingly, no police
car responded to the scene because Langley Avenue was several
miles long, and police had no way of knowing the exact address.
The next day the man told his neighbor what had happened.
The neighbor phoned the police station to complain about the
lack of police response to the theft of her clothes.

A fact largely concealed from public awareness is that
police are rather strictly policed themselves and without the
benefits of due process afforded ordinary citizens. Internal investigation and inspection units constantly observe police behavior (they too are pressured to produce "evidence" that they
are doing their job) to guard against violations of departmental

rules and regulations. Such violations range from serious graft, bribery, and corruption to petty uniform and procedural aberrations. The lore of every station house includes the times when "Joe got himself in the jackpot (got in trouble) for cussing out that drunk who turned out to be a judge's son" or "They took two (vacation) days from Mac 'cause he had rust on his handcuffs" or "They found Greg and Jack down in the park watchin' the ball game and transferred them to the Fourth District" (an undesirable "ghetto" district). Police recognize the need for internal policing mechanisms, but they resent being punished for what they feel are "chickenshit" violations.

And, as one author points out,[9] there are so many rules and regulations involved in police work that even a conscientious officer cannot help but break at least a few of them during any normal tour of duty. A free cup of coffee or a soda is a minor thing, particularly when the practice has been going on for years and has not decreased police effectiveness in the area. The behavior of the vast majority of officers does not confirm the warnings of police academy instructors that free coffee and doughnuts lead to more serious forms of graft (though it is obviously true that those officers who do wind up in serious corruption in all likelihood took a free cup of coffee now and again when they started their patrol work, just like all their non-corrupted colleagues). Most police officers will accept free food and drink only from certain trusted stores, and will not ruin the arrangement by abusing the merchant's good will. Some secretly resent the fact that their attention can be bought at all, much less so cheaply. And some never take anything without paying, not out of scrupulosity but out of a certain kind of pride and desire for autonomy.

If pressure from internal investigators is not enough, there is peer pressure in the opposite direction which, in tug-of-war fashion, increases the tension at both ends. Any police officer who wishes to gain the trust and respect of his peers must demonstrate (among other things) his willingness to thumb his nose at the administrative spirit behind minor regulations and to break certain rules. Some of this is a "hold-over" from the days when graft and pay-offs to police were so organized and widespread that almost all officers were involved to some extent. In this atmosphere, a rookie could not be trusted, and no one would speak to him with any candor for months after he came to the district. He had to win the confidence of his colleagues slowly and patiently, and this often involved establishing a record of minor violations which, if discovered, could jeopardize his job. Only when he was in a position to be "hung" himself could a new man be trusted.[10] Things are not that extreme today, but much of the old spirit remains. The pressure on a rookie can still be great.

Only four weeks out of the academy, the rookie was assigned to a radio car with a nine-year veteran who had lost his departmental driver's license as a result of a few accidents with his police cruiser. This veteran was also a stubborn man and had a reputation for being hard to get along with. They were assigned as an extra car to a post that was having a particularly high crime problem, and thus they were obligated only to patrol the area. They did not answer radio calls, except in emergencies. About halfway through the shift, the older man said to the rookie, "Let's go downtown. I gotta go to the credit union and then to a gun shop." Going downtown would have taken them several miles off their post and left them wide open for punishment should they be caught. In addition, the rookie was, like all new men, on a year's probationary status, meaning that he could (and probably would) be fired if found in any sort of major violation such as this. And the chances of being caught were not that small. The new man agonized for a few moments and told the veteran that he was not going to leave his post. The older man looked at him in disbelief and verbalized his feelings that the rookie was being a jerk. After fifteen minutes of stony silence, the man repeated his request. The rookie again declined. More stony silence. Then the man persisted in repeating his request. Looking ahead to four more hours in the same car with this officer, the rookie exploded, "Aw, goddamit!" He looked at the veteran and managed a conciliatory grin. "OK, Jed, I'll take you down there. Just understand that it's easier for you than it is for me." An hour later they were back on their post and the rookie's stomach muscles started to relax. He had made it safely.

Several months later this same rookie was asked by a different older partner to take him down to the credit union, again several miles off his assigned post as an extra car.[11] The younger officer, now a little more savvy and a little more resigned to taking risks with his job, immediately headed downtown with only a small degree of anxiety. If his sergeant called for him over the radio, or if any internal investigation units inquired about his presence so far off his post, he could say that he was en route to the city garage to have a loose fan belt fixed. When the two officers arrived at the credit union, a call came out for a bank alarm sounding back on their post. Since they did not have primary responsibility for the call, they waited to see if the alarm was for real. Most bank alarm calls are the result of employees or cleaning persons accidentally tripping the circuit. This one was for real, and they were miles away from a scene which demanded their immediate presence. The officers exchanged a knowing look. "Aw, shit," the driver muttered as he swung the cruiser around and readied himself for a high-speed race through several miles of noon-time city traffic. They must be back at the scene before their sergeant could wonder where they were. The older officer picked up the radio microphone and asked for a description of the bank robbers. This would give the impression that they were in the area searching for suspects. Twenty minutes later, with brake drums and rear tires reeking from the race uptown, the officers skirted the bank and doubled around to a nearby woods, where they left the vehicle and began a walking search of the woods. As far as anyone else was concerned, this was where they had been all along. The robbers were not apprehended, despite the presence of several police cars from neighboring posts that had not been "delayed" in their arrival. Two hours later the officers called out of service to the city garage with a "loose fan belt," and the older officer completed his trip to the credit union.[12]

The pressures on a new officer are more immediate and threatening than those on a veteran. He must gain the approval of his fellow workers, yet not alienate his sergeant by taking foolhardy or unreasonable risks in violating departmental rules. He must also not be so accommodating to older officers that they take him for a "sap" whose desire for acceptance betrays an inner weakness incompatible with the independence and "guts" needed to do the work. He must "keep his mouth shut" until such time as he feels he can be listened to as someone with something meaningful to say. Many officers mistrust or dislike a new man who bursts upon the scene full of gregariousness and instant camaraderie. Acceptance is something to be won on the street by doing one's work quietly and effectively, by "backing up" units on hazardous calls, by giving a hand with a difficult traffic accident or crime scene, and by minding one's own business. Contrary to the "crime fighter" image, large numbers of arrests are not required to demonstrate to one's colleagues that one is a "good cop." Most police recognize the considerable "luck" element involved in the well-publicized felony arrest. One must respect the integrity of another officer's decisions (regardless of private feelings, save in extreme cases of physical abuse or foolhardiness, such as a man who is about to draw his gun on a fleeing vandal); not inquire as to his relationships with merchants or other people in the district; and not intrude on his "territory" (his post) unless he requests help or it seems as though he could use it.

This may not be the ideal way of adapting oneself to policing, but it is the way things are done. Much of the petty jealousy and bristling over territorial claims by police officers seems antiquated and juvenile on the surface. But much of it is understandable. If an officer spots a "strange" police vehicle on his post, for example, he immediately thinks the worst— that internal investigators are spying on him, or that an extra car is writing up all the parking tickets on his post and thus depriving him of needed "statistics."[13] In fact, when helicopters were first introduced to police work and large identification numbers were painted on the tops of police cars, one of the greatest stumbling blocks to their acceptance was the suspicion by street patrolmen that the copters were being used to spy on them, to catch them off their posts, or sleeping in parks, or parked for "too long" a time outside certain business establishments (bars, for example).

These were—and are—pressures on older officers who had to "ride out" the technological-administrative transition in police departments over the past ten to fifteen years. They remember the days when there were only a few police cars in each district, no radios, no handcuffs, no overtime, no sick leave, and no complicated reports to write. Now they must function in a job which becomes more complex every year. They are the "old dogs" who, folk wisdom to the contrary, must indeed learn new tricks and work with young officers who may consider them unprofessional throwbacks to an era of graft and bullying. Some, admittedly, are like fish out of water in the modern police bureaucracy. But most have accumulated over the years a wealth of gut-level knowledge about mediating and intervening in human conflict and in predicting behavior on the basis of subtle attitudinal and postural cues. And, if nothing else, they have survived. Seniority alone is almost as good as rank for increasing the autonomy and respect afforded an officer. A man with, say, fifteen years or more on the job can relax a bit from the minor pressures to "produce" that fall on other officers. Supervisors, many of whom may be "hot-shot college kids" much younger than he, reserve a certain amount of awe for the experience of an older officer, however critical they may be of his style. They hesitate to carp or criticize save in extreme cases.

Any officer with more than five years' experience on the street is relatively free from the "evaluation pressure" that falls on new officers. A rookie in his probationary year is formally evaluated by his sergeant every few months, while non-probationary officers are evaluated every year. Officers with more than five years' experience have established a fairly firm reputation. If they are average, then they are accepted as average. If they are below average in their ratings, well—then they are below average, but will not be censured unless they are simply not doing the job at all. At any rate, it is a rare individual who receives a "below average" rating after five years in the department. Not only are supervisors reluctant to put down on paper criticisms of their officers (sergeants will often give a high rating to a man who they privately feel is doing a poor job; in these cases, they will attempt to improve the man's performance without putting any detrimental material in his personnel folder), but people just do not last that long if they are so willing to alienate their sergeant that he is forced to formalize his criticism on a departmental rating form.

Officers out of probation but with less than five years' ex-

perience[14] still must either prove or disprove their capacities for
leadership, responsibility, initiative, ambition, enthusiasm, and
dedication to the job. They are no longer subject to disciplinary
dismissal without a hearing, as are probationary officers, but
they still must prove their mettle for the long haul ahead. This
is the crucial period for promotions, schooling, and political
maneuvering for prime assignments.

Probationary officers are, in effect, evaluated every minute
they are on the job. Every situation is a test of the new officer's
judgment, attitudes, and "common sense"—that catch-all phrase
for the ability to see things in the normative perspective and
respond with approved behaviors in the absence of any overt
coaching.[15] In a job where experience counts so much, inexperience is an inherently damning condition. The rookie's exas-
peration is exacerbated by the failure of most police departments
to institutionalize and thus facilitate his entrance into the working world of his (potential) colleagues. Some departments are
beginning to help the new officer by pairing him with older
officers who have volunteered to teach him the police craft.
But by and large the only reminders he gets that he is not yet
a full-fledged "member of the crew" are negative ones. In an
official respect, his probationary status means that his job can
be taken away from him at any time with no explanation by the
department (the fact that this is rarely done does not decrease
his anxiety that it *might* happen to him). Unofficially, he must
rely on his own interpersonal skills to feel his way through the
subtle, non-verbal acceptance process. If, for example, he finds
himself shut out of conversations, or if no one wants to help
him out with a report, or if people let him make mistakes when
they could have said something to him to prevent the mistakes,
then he is being sent a message—probably that he is not behaving humbly enough to be taught by his elders and will therefore have to learn the hard way.

Because the ability to do police work depends, in part, on
what officers consider an "innate" capacity for dealing with
people, there is little attempt to instruct the new officer in anything but departmental procedures and district geography.
Bittner notes that the net result is that "the same demands are
made of barely initiated officers as are made of experienced

practitioners. Correspondingly, beginners tend to think that they can do as well as their more knowledgeable peers. As this leads to inevitable frustrations, they find themselves in a situation that is conducive to the development of a particular sense of 'touchiness.' Personal dispositions of officers are, of course, of great relevance. But the license of discretionary freedom and the expectation of success under conditions of autonomy, without any indication that the work of the successful craftsman is based on an acquired preparedness for the task, is ready-made for failure and malpractice. Moreover, it leads to slipshod practices of patrol that also infect the standards of the careful craftsman."[16]

A rookie must make up for these disadvantages by admitting ignorance and seeking help when necessary. Yet he must not appear ineffective or indecisive. For the prompt and appropriate exercise of powerful discretion is another central feature of policing, and calling for assistance is as much a reflection on one's discretionary capabilities as is the manner in which one handles the substantive matter at hand. New officers are expected to make procedural mistakes, and these are easily corrected and forgiven. But mistakes that call into question one's judgment about people or one's decisiveness under stress are not as easily forgiven—or forgotten.

Some female patrol officers I have worked with have trouble on this score (I am referring to those women assigned as regular street patrol officers) because they do not, understandably, share the unspoken, unwritten perspectives of an action-oriented "male" occupation. One such rookie, for example, stopped a vehicle for a traffic violation and discovered that the driver did not have on his person either his driver's license or the registration to the car. Sensing that it was not a stolen car, the officer prepared to fill out a traffic ticket but found herself unable to do so without the information usually obtained from the license and registration. She radioed for her sergeant to meet her and advise her as to what she should do. Now, in terms of departmental procedures, academy training, and the like, she was certainly making no mistakes. But according to the unspoken mores of patrol officers,[17] she was committing three errors. First, she was "bothering" her sergeant with a petty matter—a traffic citation—which she should have been able to take care of herself. Second, she was admitting her ignorance of procedure directly to a supervisor when she could have found out what she needed to know from a like-ranked colleague. And third, she was potentially involving her sergeant in a borderline legal decision as to the fate of the driver. Other officers in the same position would probably have let the driver go with a verbal warning, not so much out of mercy as out of procedural ignorance. But once the sergeant is called, he is put in the position of condoning or altering any decision the officer makes and therefore must share the consequences with the officer. Officers respectfully do not burden their "sarge" with petty decision-making because they know he will have to bear some of the responsibility for their decisions in major incidents. Letting a traffic violator off with a verbal warning is a minor discretionary decision. An officer who cannot make such decisions without the sergeant's help is likely to be equally helpless in situations calling for more weighty judgments, and thus becomes a burden to colleagues and supervisors.

One may think there is something wrong with this arrangement, or that it is not particularly fair. Supervisors should be able and willing to assist novices and should even take extra care to insure that a new officer is learning in a fairly comfortable way. As it is, sergeants often are concerned only about whether or not the new officer might cause embarrassment, or censure, to the squad or to themselves. Though some altruistic and instructional concern is present, their primary concern is more often one of protecting themselves from the rashness or stupidity of the innocent. If female officers do not "catch on" to the unwritten subculture and the unspoken assumptions, they are often written off as "bad police material." But many new male officers go through the same confusion, and the "sink-or-swim" attitude of many departments toward rookie officers seems designed to maximize feelings of shock, uncertainty, and inadequacy. Departmental hostility toward women patrol officers aggravates these feelings for them.

Since female patrol officers are still rare, little in the way of systematic research has been done to assess their effectiveness or competence. However, a 1974 study by the Police Foundation in Washington, D.C., reports: "The survey compared 86 male with 86 female officers on the Capitol's police force for a year and found little difference in the abilities of men and women to deal with violent or potentially violent situations. Women were found to be similar or equal to men in the percentage of arrests they made that resulted in conviction, their attitude toward the public, the number of incidents they were involved in that required back-up support from other officers, the number of injuries they sustained on the job, and even the number of driving accidents they had. Perhaps the most annoying on-the-job irritant women officers faced: hostility from male officers." [18]

Future research will probably confirm these findings. However, there is a tendency for police and non-police alike to focus on a female's handling of physical incidents when judgments are being made about her competence. Effective policing involves not only the ability to deal with the public and with the service calls one receives, but also the ability to form good working relationships with one's colleagues. Often through no fault of her own, the female patrol officer has great difficulty on this count. The subculture of policing includes many culturally "male" elements such as defensiveness concerning personal courage and territorial claims, the reluctance to admit failure or ignorance, and "hardness" in the presence of emotional stimulation. The whole concept of "being a man" has meaning for policemen, for it sums up a lot of unverbalized feelings they have about what it takes to do the job and earn the respect of other men. At this time women are being evaluated according to some "unisex" model of efficiency, whereas the evaluations made by colleagues stem from the "male" model of the job. The situation is set up for bad feelings to surface, particularly since policemen are easily sidetracked into discussions of the physical competence of females without fully realizing the extent to which male characteristics other than the muscular enter into their occupational identity.

Present discussion of female patrol officers often generates more heat than light, with much of the heat coming from male officers. It helps to keep in mind here that there have always been a few men in traditionally female occupations and a few women in traditionally male occupations, including policing. That women want to expand their usual role within police departments is no more surprising than their desire to become ordained priests, telephone linemen, or bus drivers. And the expected opposition from the ranks is no more surprising for male police than for male bishops or male bus drivers. The changes occurring have broad social causes and will not be stopped by male grumpiness alone. At the same time, sex roles are fairly well-established in most of us, and whatever changes occur are not likely to be numerically sweeping or hermaphroditic in their effects. In the future as in the past, most police officers are likely to be male.

The main instructional value of this whole issue, therefore, lies not in describing or justifying the "revolutionary" attitudes of women or the defensive attitudes of men. It lies rather in discovering the extent to which occupational and sexual identities often become fused, and the extent to which people inject into their work powerful feelings of sex-specific pride and fulfillment. To recognize that these feelings bear little or no relation to the job as such is not to surrender one's sexual identity, but to clarify one's occupational identity. If female officers do little more than help male officers to divest their patrol activities of unnecessary and often counterproductive machismo, they will have advanced the profession considerably. A man trying to cope with the pressures of policing does not need the additional pressures of trying to be a "John Wayne."

So great are the pressures on new officers, and so great is their desire for acceptance into the police subculture, that a good bit of "anticipatory socialization" takes place in the police academy, months before the new officer actually reaches the streets. Through contacts with instructors in more candid moments, with friends and relatives who are police officers, and through the intangible grapevine, rookies learn the attitudes, philosophy, and biases of their new group. They pick up a certain mistrust and hostility toward the news media, lenient judges, civil libertarians, and "social workers" (a generic term used to describe anyone whose purpose is to change rather than punish criminal behavior). They adopt a general suspicion of the public and learn that they can probably expect the worst from it. In time, of course, what was once anticipatory becomes genuine, and young policemen become more solidified in their not-too-pleasant conception of mankind. They come to see the world as a very physical sort of place where people fight, scream, shoot, mug, rape, beat their wives, batter their children, crash their automobiles, ruin property, and get bitten by dogs. The service revolver, initially sticking out like a sore thumb in the rookie's self-consciousness, gradually becomes an exceedingly appropriate thing to carry around on the streets of our cities. It feels comfortable, and its presence is a symbol to others and to himself that he can handle violence. The new officer may enjoy this new responsibility and power, but he will not really fathom its depth and nature until he finds himself a hair's breadth from using it. After his knees once more solidify beneath him and he has controlled his fear and anger, he will have to rethink his role and his commitment to meeting violence on its own terms.[19]

Until that moment (and after, too, if he can come to terms with his own capacity for violence), he will find himself sharing in the police subculture with a gratifying sense of having "made it." He is part of the group. But once he accepts the realities of violence and the realities of his own response to it, he will not so much adopt the pessimistic police philosophy as it will adopt him. The cynicism will deepen and harden, almost beyond his control, and the use of force will become a simple fact of life, to be debated and discussed by people who do not know the depth and character of their own impulses, much less those of others. The police subculture will become a protective shell of mutual understanding, uniting police as it isolates them from a public that "doesn't understand."

There is, of course, a certain amount of hurt-little-boy pouting involved in this self-isolation of police.[20] Granted that our need as a society to deny the magnitude of our violence is great, it is not so great as to block communication between ourselves and our police. But first we must recognize the fact that we have set our police up to be the agents both of our violence and of our denial. We have charged them with the task of making our streets safe while we close our eyes and hope for the best. And having done this, we turn around in our

movies and television shows to create police who do not defuse
violence, or sweep it under the rug, but act it out against "bad
guys" whose obliteration confirms our fantasies of how crime
fighting should be conducted.

We must do much thinking about the disturbingly central
place of violence in our fantasies and our entertainment. We
must worry about our national boredom, and whether we are
allowing ourselves to become desensitized to all but the most
graphic sorts of sadism. And we should do these things with our
police, for they embody many rejected elements of our own
lives and assume a strongly defensive posture toward criticism
and insight.

What is hidden from public view, however, is the fact that
police are united only by their occupational identity and the
authority of their job. There is as much back-biting, gossip, and
petty intrigue around a police station as there is anywhere else.
The autonomy of police (once away from the station and on
their own posts) and their wide discretionary powers make for
several different and often conflicting styles of policing. Every
officer can to a great extent shape his job according to his own
conceptions of order, law, and public peace. And remember that
police are used to getting their own way. They are used to having people conform to their demands. They expect compliance
from citizens, and their ready exercise of authority day after day
does not help them to become compromising or willing to "live
and let live." So when an officer who stringently enforces traffic
laws works in the same car as an officer who does not, conflict
will arise because each man is so used to imposing his own
interpretation of proper behavior on others. In addition, the
failure of police to recognize publicly the facts of discretionary
enforcement encourages in some officers the idea that there *is*
really only one way to do the job—their way.

The subject of police unions further highlights the individuality of officers and suggests that there is less homogeneity
and in-grouping than one might expect. Efforts to unionize police
have met with patchy success, and police are divided over the
desirability and necessity of unions. Furthermore, even where
the need for representation is recognized, there is conflict over
who can represent most adequately—fraternal organizations

(such as the Fraternal Order of Police), local government employees unions, or national unions like the Teamsters. This conflict can at times become quite stressful.

My last few months in the department saw a referendum by the officers on whether or not to strike. Finally, those officers belonging to the union (in this case a local government employees union) did decide to go out on strike.

The issues were fairly commonplace (including low pay and inadequate benefits), but feelings ran very high. The police commissioner was determined to break the strike and felt that the national reputation of the department and his own reputation as a leader were at stake. Moreover, he believed that if police could strike successfully in one city, they could do so in other cities. Thus he felt pressured by other administrators across the country to nip this epidemic in the bud.

Officers were divided unequally between those supporting the strike (the majority) and those who were against it. It was an ugly two-week strike, with union members picketing station houses, spitting on or kicking patrol cars as non-striking officers departed for duty, and occasionally brandishing weapons and beer cans on the picket lines. State police were called in to supplement patrols, and supervisory officers worked overtime trying to make up for lost manpower. Friendships were broken. The complex web of supporting arrangements between men who suspend differences to work on a common task was torn apart. There were good and competent officers on both sides of the argument, but there was nothing but punitiveness, panic, and retaliation from the top command.

The strike was eventually settled, but in its aftermath came a veritable bureaucratic holocaust. Captains in districts whose officers had struck were relieved of their commands, as if they had been responsible for the whole business. All probationary officers in the department who had honored the strike were summarily dismissed. Some were subsequently hired by adjacent county departments or left police work altogether. I had the good fortune to be called away on military reserve training for the two weeks of the strike, and this coincidence spared me an agonizing decision. My entire squad struck. What would you have done? How could you have functioned after the strike if you had driven your green self in a patrol car past a picket line composed of your teachers, mentors, friends, and colleagues?

The settlement netted some gains in salary and benefits for all officers and thus further alienated those who had struck from those who stayed on the job. I should note here that many of those who struck came from blue-collar families and had fathers who had spent years toiling in a mine or factory. These men had strong feelings about the necessity of unions and the ease with which persons in authority can abuse employees. For them, policing was a clean, secure job and represented a step upward from their fathers' situations. Their disillusionment with policing and its rewards was thus aggravated by their initial expectations.

This strike occurred in the summer of 1974. In the summer of 1977, I heard over the radio that twenty-two of the probationary patrolmen fired for honoring picket lines were suing the union on the grounds that it failed to protect them from the consequences of the strike.

The subject of unions is a far-ranging one, and it is not noted for generating dispassionate discussion. The old feeling · that professionals are above unionization has given way to the feeling that professionals are as likely as anyone else to get the short end of the stick. Groups that years ago would not have thought of picketing have found the strike to be a useful tool. These groups include medical interns, teachers, and nurses —and police officers. What should be noted for our purposes are the dynamics of unionization. Involved are collective patterns of defense in response to abuse or pressure, out of which come collective activities to change or thwart the perceived abuse. The abuse is felt to be inherent in the employee-employer relationship and therefore must always be suspect. The union thus becomes a permanent organization.

When employees unionize or talk of unionization, they are saying that they experience their working environment as hostile and unsupportive, and that their employers or managers (usually called "bosses") are misunderstanding and untrustworthy. Since no one really has their best interests at heart, they must fight for things that at one time may have come willingly out of the employers' sense of responsibility or "noblesse oblige."

The relationship between workers and employer is reduced to a cold, calculated, chronically hostile quid pro quo in which milligrams of effort are carefully measured out for milligrams of reward. Exchange is gruff and basically without satisfaction. Financial compensation and a list of benefits can become the only sources of job satisfaction. The paycheck itself takes on new meaning as something conceded reluctantly in response to collective pressure rather than something given in gratitude for a job well done.

That such a situation could exist in a police department is alarming, and constitutes at the very least an undesirable source of pressure and antagonism for patrolmen.

There are also many extradepartmental pressures on police. Shift work is one. The officer does not see his family as much as most people. And his wife generally will not be happy with his job choice, not so much because it is dangerous (there are many jobs that are more dangerous, including lumberjack and anthracite coal miner), but because it tends to harden a man and make him less loving and lovable. He cannot afford to indulge his feelings on the job because his responsibilities are great and involve cool thinking in the midst of traumatic events. His emotional reactions to these events are often delayed and sometimes do not appear at all.[21] When he comes home (if his wife is still awake, or not out shopping or taking the kids to school), he has nothing particularly pleasant to tell her. She does not want to hear about his disorderly conduct arrests, or the traffic tickets he gave out, or the corpse someone discovered on the other side of town. And neither do his neighbors and friends. They recognize the need for police and are glad that someone takes the job. But that does not mean that they want to hear about it. An officer's friends turn out to be those who can transcend stereotypes, or turn out to be other police.

A detective and an officer knocked on the door of the old but well-built wood house in a deteriorating section of the city. They were dressed in plainclothes—ragged jeans and old sweaters—and were looking for an eighteen-year-old boy who had bought a stolen motorcycle from one of his friends. The boy's mother, a nurse in one of the city hospitals, answered the door and allowed the officers to come in. They explained their purpose, and the woman managed a wan smile. "You know," she said, "you two are dressed very à propos. But . . . somehow . . . you can always smell a cop, you know? You can *smell* that cop." She dragged the words out slowly, feigning (?) a slight nausea at the fact that two "cops" were in her house emanating psychic odors of some kind.

Police know that this attitude, if a bit extreme, is not rare. They feel that most people do not like police, and so they assume many of the standard defensive and counter-aggressive attitudes of outcast minority groups. They are, paradoxically, in much the same position as the blacks whom they are so often accused of persecuting. Both blacks and police live in a somewhat hypocritical public environment. People voice one opinion in front of them and another behind their backs. Even those who appear friendly cannot be trusted. The black person cannot escape this condition because his pigment is permanent. But a policeman can take off his uniform and "mingle," and he often hears snide or contemptuous comments about "pigs" or the "goddamn cops." He gets less subtle reminders of societal attitudes than many black people get.[22]

As with blacks, the social status of police is not high. In fact, the farther police are removed from contact with black people, the higher their pay and status. There is a rough progression from city police to county police to state troopers to federal agents. And, in general, the standards for acceptance increase along this progression too. City police are conscious of their lack of status. Some shrug it off as irrelevant to their well-being. Others regard themselves as lucky to have a secure, steady job—status or no status. But many, especially younger, officers are touchy on this subject. They are "police officers," not "cops." They are law enforcement professionals, and often they have taken or are taking courses in criminology and police science at local colleges to advance their careers and gain a wider perspective on their work. Their older, pot-bellied, easy-going colleagues embarrass them and have little to offer a professionalized department. Even their language becomes stilted as they adopt the bureaucratese of the profession.

A young black officer walked into a corner liquor store in a poor neighborhood one Saturday evening. Half a dozen local winos were draped over a nearby railing, and small children were playing noisily around the entrance to the store. Music blared from an upstairs window. The officer had received a call for a fight at that address. But no one seemed to notice him as he approached the thick, yellowed plexiglass that separated the storeowner and his wares from the customers. He walked up to the opening in the glass and asked stiffly, "Did anyone here request police services?" The owner looked quizzically at him and mumbled, "Naw, we didn't call for no cops. But try next door. Them fuckin' people fight all the time."

Young black police can, understandably, be more sensitive than others to the issue of professionalism and status. Striving to make it in the expanding black middle class, they find themselves caught up in the white-collar-and-tie syndrome wherein anyone who leaves for work in the morning carrying an attaché case and an unexplainable job title has succeeded in life. They leave for work at all hours of the day and night, and often patrol the despised ghettos they have worked so hard to escape or avoid.[23] It is harder for them to indulge their success fantasies of life in the technocratic paradise under these conditions. By the same token, they often (but by no means always) are able to see ghetto residents in humanitarian and sympathetic ways—a difficult task for someone who does not, or does not want to, understand the ways and means of poor Americans.

The position of black officers is unique, but in many ways it is merely a magnification of the position of many other officers. Promotion is becoming more and more difficult as the qualifications of police candidates increase in number and stringency. A college degree is still a little unusual in many police departments, but it is not at all unusual for an officer to be working toward his degree, aided by funds from the Law Enforcement Assistance Administration in Washington, D.C. Competition is getting keener, and frustrations are going to rise as more qualified men charge for a foothold on the bureaucratic ladder. The alienated quality of work and the deceptive lures of success affect police as much as they affect other groups, if not more so. For police are, in many respects, the "niggers" of the working world. Their job is shrouded in a mythology of negativism and futility. The work has its lures, obviously, but the overall picture defines policing as a job fit only for those who cannot get promoted out of it. Police become so convinced of the undesirability of street patrol that they often try hard to detach themselves from it through reassignment, advancement, or the adoption of less active styles of patrolling. And when they fail, their self-reproach and loss of esteem can be shattering. Do not forget that many of these men believe ghettos to be populated by people who lack the ambition or intelligence to escape. The implications of their own failure to escape can be frightening indeed.

In addition to the intra- and extradepartmental pressures mentioned above, there are pressures inherent in the work itself, quite apart from the machinations of the police bureaucracy or the attitudes of the public. Violence and fighting are stressful, if only to witness or clean up after. Boredom and routine are also stressful. Officers who sleep on the midnight shift do so not so much because they are tired as because it is the fastest way of passing the time. In the not-so-distant past, officers would engage in petty thievery or sex with trusted prostitutes to keep themselves occupied during the "graveyard" shift.[24] Some officers enjoy this shift. Generally, they are the "gung-ho" type who either enjoy picking off the traffic violations that occur in the dead of night, or assume that anyone on the streets after 2:00 A.M. must be up to no good and is therefore worthy of their investigation.

Most officers look forward to daywork not because of the work, but because it allows them to live a normal life at home for a few weeks. They can see their kids, go to a P.T.A. meeting, take their wives to a movie, or go shopping like a normal person keeping normal hours. Daywork itself is not liked by many officers. There are petty, bothersome duties such as bank checks, school crossings, and vehicle maintenance to be performed. Police are highly visible in the daytime and cannot "hide" in a park or behind a store to get some peace and quiet for a few moments. Someone is always watching them, even when they eat lunch, and someone always seems anxious to intrude and "bend their ear" over neighborhood or personal problems. There are more "mental cases" on the street than most people realize, and while these people in a general sense are indistinguishable from other people, they often relate to police in unusual or annoying ways. Because it is often a police officer who takes these people into custody and thus starts the process of institutional commitment, the officer is seen as part of the whole helping or incarcerating (depending on one's point of view) mechanism and thus can be approached anywhere at any time to listen to complaints or symptoms.

But a person need not have a history of psychiatric hospitalization to become an annoyance to police. Old folks—abandoned by their families, widowed, or otherwise left alone—will insist on telling the officer all about their former careers, their grandchildren, their ailments, or the strange comings and goings they see from behind their windows. The officer is approached by almost everyone as an anonymous official, a body filling a uniform whose personal identity is an irrelevance. People do not bother to introduce themselves before speaking to him. He comes to feel like a one-man institution, impersonal and abusable. Like pens and pencils in a large office, his good will and skills are taken for granted. He starts to reciprocate, and does not really care about the lives of the people who talk to him anonymously because they do not particularly care about him. He becomes a master at "bowing out" of conversations on some pretext so he can return to the privacy and definition of his streets.

But on daywork, even when he is not burdened with unwanted "interpersonalizing," the sun glares into his eyes and he finds it hard to get car stops and traffic violations. People drive carefully in the presence of his visible cruiser. He cannot look for a taillight out, or a headlight. There are fewer teens on the road during the day. And he must negotiate the traffic of supermarket shoppers and errand-runners, many of whom drive so poorly and unpredictably (because of age, inexperience, or the presence of distracting small children) that they dare to drive only during the mid-morning hours.

The night shift (four-to-twelve) provides the officer with most of his memorable experiences and challenges. Most marital conflicts occur at night and on weekends simply because husbands and wives are together during these times. Teenagers are on the streets, at once the most bored, restless, and idle group in our society. People have always taken advantage of darkness to burglarize, assault, or victimize their fellows, and there is something about the quality of night itself which seems to stimulate passion and impulses dormant in the light of day. An officer can rest peacefully in a darkened spot out of the public eye and have a cup of coffee or a sandwich. Yet he can hear over his radio the litany of unrest and conflict that drones over the city. He is safe amidst the chaos of others, and he is privy to a knowledge of city life that few others share.

There is little or no boredom on this shift, and statistics are easily accumulated. Car stops and traffic violations are plentiful, and there are ample opportunities to solidify relationships by backing up colleagues on dangerous calls. It is on this shift, primarily, that an officer discovers whether or not he has what it takes to police. It is here that he will encounter the extremes of hostility, cruelty, and danger. If he enjoys his work, his response will be one of fear, anticipation, eagerness, and aggression, all carefully orchestrated to produce an attitude of controlled assertiveness. If he is not reasonably afraid, he is either emotionally blunted or stupid. If he is not eager, then he does not have that hunger for risky encounters necessary for effective patrol. If he is not capable of anger, he will not be able to retaliate when attacked. And if he is not controlled, his fear and anger will get away from him and he will lose, at the very least, the trust and respect of his co-workers.

Control is a key word in policing. Not only is a competent officer highly self-controlled. He is also willing and able to control others and to take command of a situation. He is "the man." He is the one who has to sort out the often confusing elements at a crime scene, accident, or crowd disturbance and arrive at a decision, even if the most appropriate decision he can make is to call his supervisor.

Most police officers see themselves as individualists. Even if they work with a partner, they see themselves as taking full responsibility for their decisions. They take all the flack for their mistakes (though the bureaucracy through its "chain of command" will also hold a supervisor responsible for his subordinates' decisions), and they do not expect anyone to go to bat for them if they get into some sort of jam with the public or with departmental investigators. A new officer is told, or rather warned, several times in the academy and in his district to "look out for number one" (himself). Thus, when an officer transports a rape victim to the hospital for examination and treatment, he reports to the dispatcher over the radio both his starting time and mileage and his arrival time and mileage so that no allegations can be made by the victim that the officer took liberties with her en route to the hospital. All radio conversations are recorded on a continuously running tape recorder and are stored for a period of thirty days before being erased. This record of all dispatched calls and responses can be examined in the event of citizen complaints about the lack of police response. This procedure also discourages abuse of the radio by officers, for the idea of a permanent record of any kind (thirty days is permanent enough in police work) instills caution. Some cities have gone so far as to take a "voiceprint" of all officers so that wisecracks and obscenities aired on the radio can be traced to the man who voiced them. There are persons in every district who will "spy" on police and telephone headquarters to report alleged misconduct or laxity. One old man used to take Polaroid pictures of officers eating lunch in their cars, hoping that the time of their lunch did not correspond to the time they called out for lunch over the radio. In time, of course, internal investigators get to know these "cranks" and ignore their eccentricities. But enough "average" citizens complain about their police that officers are suspicious and wary of all but familiar persons.

In this sort of work environment, backing up other officers on calls takes on an added meaning. Not only does it offer assistance. It also demonstrates a willingness to look out for a colleague when no one else seems to care. So valued and respected is this willingness that officers will overlook considerable obnoxiousness and unfriendliness in a co-worker if he is the type who will go out of his way to "back them up" on dangerous calls. (Remember in this regard that the officer who does the backing up frequently arrives at the scene before the primary officer, and thus becomes the primary candidate for injury should things go awry. It is not unusual to receive a call for, say, a robbery-in-progress, and arrive at the scene within minutes to find the entire area covered with officers from tactical and other units who did not bother to notify the dispatcher that they were responding.)

A call in which an officer was fatally shot dramatizes the extent to which officers feel they cannot count on administrators to stand by them under fire. The officer had answered a call for a "man with a gun" in a house, and had been backed up by another car. When he entered the house, he was greeted by a shotgun blast that struck him and his partner. He dragged his partner out the door to safety and collapsed in the front yard. He died a month later in the hospital from massive post-operative infections. After he and his partner had escaped from the house, a siege began in which more than a dozen officers surrounded the place and attempted to get a shot at the man inside. After an hour he surrendered and was taken to jail. The chief of the patrol division was on the scene, and his only comment when the whole sordid business was over was a public criticism of his men for unbuttoning their coats and removing their hats during the gun battle. He also seemed to think that their guns had been drawn unnecessarily. (In fact, patrol officers are often advised to remove their hats in situations like this because the shiny hatpiece makes an excellent target!) This administrator's comments caused such a stir among police and sympathetic citizens that he was transferred to another position within the department.

In light of their conviction that they can rely only on other patrolmen (this includes patrol sergeants, lieutenants, detectives, and sometimes district captains who have proven that they will back their men) for help, it is a wonder that officers daily assume the risks they do.

After blowing most of his girlfriend's head off with a shotgun, a man ran into a wooded area that was growing darker in the Friday twilight. There was a good possibility that he was hiding in an abandoned house in the center of a small clearing in the woods. Four officers decided to search the house. Three were young, ranging in experience from three months to four years, while one had seventeen years with the department. The "older" officer (thirty-eight years old) took the shotgun out of the trunk of his cruiser and headed into the basement of the house, followed by the other three. All had their guns drawn and pointed into the air to guard against shooting each other if any surprise caused fingers to twitch suddenly. As the least experienced officer followed the shotgun up the stairs and around the rooms and closets, he was shocked by the reality of the risks taken by all, but especially by the older man. He had insisted on going first with the shotgun (perhaps he trusted himself more than the younger men with this terrible weapon), and around any corner or crouching in any closet might be a man who in his terror would not think twice about slaughtering the father of three children who had only three years to go before enjoying a long and well-deserved retirement. As things turned out, the man was not in the house and had apparently escaped through the woods. The shotgun went back in the trunk, and the men resumed patrol.

CHAPTER 5

Styles of Policing

WHAT I MEAN by "style" of policing is the characteristic way an officer exercises his discretionary enforcement powers. This style is shaped by multiple situational and personal factors, such as the values and priorities (and "personality") of the individual officer, the demands of the work, and the various pressures brought to bear on an officer. Around the station house it is a recognized fact that some men are "aggressive" patrolmen while others "just plain don't give a damn." Some are "traffic men." Some concentrate aggressively on juvenile offenders but go easy on adults, and vice-versa. Some "go by the book." Some avoid work, some seek it out.

Because of the ambiguities inherent in the job, there is ample room for the injection of individual ideas of how the work is to be done. No two police officers work in the same way. No two react identically in all situations. They are as different on the job as they are off the job. But in spite of the ideographic nature of policing, some generalities can be suggested to bring different styles into clearer focus. Wilson, for example, maintains that entire departments can be classified as having a "watchman," "legalistic," or a "service" style.[1]

I will suggest five styles of individual policing: "safe,"

"producing," "crime fighting," "avoiding," and "street policing."
This schema is not intended to be exhaustive, nor will every
officer fit neatly into any one category. But it is hoped that the
styles presented will be sufficiently descriptive to stimulate further examination and discussion.[2]

As the name implies, the "safe" officer plays it safe. He
does not rock any boats. His primary interest in his job is
likely to be the security of a pension at the end of twenty years'
service, and he does not wish to jeopardize this pension by going
out on a limb. He follows departmental regulations as closely
as he can without losing the trust of his fellow officers. He
avoids contact with "higher-ups," does not actively seek administrative responsibility or promotion, and does not go out of
his way to investigate crime or pursue criminals. He will, of
course, do his job, and this alone will involve considerable risks
and much aggressive activity such as stopping suspicious vehicles and responding to felony-in-progress calls. But when it
comes to that "something extra" which would earn him a promotion to detective or a special commendation, he is likely to
think it a valueless effort with unnecessary risks, and he will
leave it alone. He tries his best to "tone down" the anger and
conflict he encounters on the street, and uses his power to
arrest sparingly. He is generally kinder, more sensitive, and
more peaceful to be with than most officers. His heart is not
really in the job, but in the stability and financial security that
the job brings. When he joined the police department, he probably craved a little excitement and perhaps even a touch of
desired manhood. But the job turned sour somewhere along the
line, and he cynically (or wisely) decided to walk the line between filling the demands of the job and not making any waves.
The safe officer finds all his worst fears and anxieties about the
job summed up in incidents such as the following:

It was 1:30 in the morning when the radio put out a
description of three men who had just robbed a carry-out at
gunpoint and escaped in a car. Three officers closed in on the
car after spotting it on a cross-town thoroughfare. When it
careened to a halt along the side of the road, two men jumped
out and made good their escape through a nearby woods. But
the third man was too slow, and emerged to face an officer's

cocked revolver. Then something went wrong. The officer for some reason or other switched the revolver from one hand to the other, and in the process the gun discharged. The bullet went through the officer's thigh, ricocheted off the street, and struck the other two officers, one in the shin and the other in the finger. The discharge had been accidental, and all wounds were superficial, or at least not terribly serious. But the officers, because of their conviction that the officer responsible would lose his job over the incident (he was in his probationary year), agreed on a story: the prisoner had grabbed for the gun and in the struggle it had gone off. They wrote their report this way, and the prisoner was charged with three counts of assault with attempt to murder in addition to the armed robbery charge. But the report these officers wrote contradicted the report written by police from a neighboring jurisdiction who had also responded to the call, and the officers were eventually grilled by internal investigators. Two (the two older men) stuck by their story. But the third—the probationary officer whose gun had fired —could not stick by the false story through a trial, under oath, and send a man to prison for attempted murder. He "cracked" and was fired. The other two men were forced to resign, and the whole story received much publicity in local newspapers for about three days.

In the safe officer's mind, trouble begets trouble. In the words of one such officer who reacted to the above incident, "Oh, what a tangled web we weave when we first practice to deceive." In the above incident, he would not have cocked his revolver, for it takes very little pressure to fire a cocked gun. If through some miscalculation the gun *had* discharged, he would not have complicated matters further by falsifying a report. In extreme cases of safe policing, an officer would have calculated his arrival so as to be too late to apprehend the robbers, or to arrive after others had the situation under control. But only very frightened officers, or officers very close to retirement, will make a habit of this tactic (though many will consider it). Reputations are established quickly in police work, are almost impossible to change, and are paramount in determining what sort of respect and friendship (and help) one can expect from one's colleagues.

The safe officer is usually (but not always) an older officer who has grown rather philosophical about crime over the years. He has seen countless criminals go unapprehended. He has seen them walk out of our overcrowded prisons on premature probations, only to commit the same crimes over and over again. He has seen enough of human nature to know that "crime fighting" is as futile as it is foolhardy. He will be damned if he will risk his neck so that a criminal can be apprehended, tried, and returned to the streets on a suspended sentence.[3] He can be deeply cynical and pessimistic, and often spends a lot of time daydreaming about a peaceful, conflict-free retirement. His attitude toward the enthusiasm he imagines to run rampant in all rookies is one of amused tolerance, tinged slightly with bitterness and a sense of loss.

The young officer was fresh out of the academy—his second day in the district. He had been assigned to Herb, a seventeen-year veteran, who would show him around the district. Herb, like most safe officers, enjoyed teaching a younger man the "ropes," and was a solicitous and patient teacher. As they rode through a busy shopping district, the new man looked with eagerness on the crowds and the stores. Perhaps the veteran caught the old feeling of excitement. He turned to his new partner and said, "You know, when I first came out here I was all full of piss and vinegar too. You couldn't stop me. And that's OK, you know? You always start out that way. But I tell ya . . . after a while maybe you learn to take things a little easier. You go to all this trouble, bustin' your ass 'n' all, and what do you get? You learn to relax a little bit—take things as they come. You last longer that way."

The "aggressive" quality that these officers bring to their patrol work is often more apparent than real. For example, on sighting a speeding car, a safe officer may swing his car around abruptly, roar away in pursuit, and negotiate traffic signals, autos, and other obstacles to pull over the offender. If you were present in such a situation (common though it is), you might assume the officer to be angry, vindictive, tense, or annoyed. You would, then, be surprised at the almost impassive air of the safe officer as he hands out an ordinary ticket in an ordinary situation with no sense of rancor or vengeance.

Other officers with other styles may present a very different picture, as we shall see. But the safe officer carries out his basic duties and responsibilities with a minimum of fuss and emotional involvement. His heart is at home with his wife, his kids, and the things he has worked hard for. It is not unusual for these things to form the bulk of his conversation during a shift. It would be inaccurate to say that he dislikes his job. By the same token, he would probably agree that it is "just" a job. Very often, the material and familial comforts made possible by his paycheck serve as sufficient rationale for his continuance in police work.

In some cases the adoption of the safe style has defensive origins. I recall one officer of five years' experience—a warm and mild-mannered man—who had incurred a back injury in a departmental auto accident during his probationary year. His injuries had not been disabling, but the medical costs and recuperation period had both been extensive. The department had tried to fire him during this time (concerned, perhaps, about continuing an officer with a potential for future medical expenses and much sick leave), and he had successfully fought the effort. The experience embittered him, however, and when I knew him he was walking a dull but permanent foot post in a lower-middle-class, stable area. He had twin daughters whom he loved dearly, but his moonlighting as a security guard to provide extra income meant that he hardly ever saw them. He never told me, but I suspected his marriage might be shaky. One could predict that the fifteen years until his retirement will be a feat of considerable endurance.

Because they are sensitive, steady, and chary of involvement in the frustrating machinery of the law, these officers are often more skilled than others at resolving tensions, arguments, and even legal violations with a minimum of complication. A new officer might easily see them as timid, lazy, or soft. However, the frequency of this style suggests that it is not so much a retreat from duty as an adaptation to pressures felt as hostile and capricious, whether originating inside or outside the department.

A second style of policing is the "producing" style. The producer is not as philosophical as his safe colleague, and generally they do not get along well together. The producer takes his job requirements quite literally and enforces the law in a narrow, legalistic fashion. He does not like ambiguity and would (if he could) remove much of the discretionary judgment from police work. He removes as much as he can from his own work by applying the law in a clumsy, egalitarian way. He is most at home in a statistically-oriented department, and seeks the relative clarity of numerical performance standards. He enjoys accumulating more car stops, business checks, field interviews, arrests, parking tickets, and moving violations than his colleagues. Through this, he gains some sense of accomplishment, some feeling that after eight hours on the street he has actually "done something." He has a strong need for tangible, concrete results, and a disdain for cultivating interpersonal relationships.

Producers often wind up in traffic enforcement divisions within departments, for the voluminous traffic code, when taken literally, provides ample opportunity for accumulating paperwork and statistics.

Producers do not often advance out of patrol work. They do not, in general, get promoted very quickly. Their willingness to alienate others in the name of enforcement earns them few friends, either inside or outside the department. And their heavy-handedness in interpersonal relations means they do not have the adaptiveness and sensitivity to others' needs that are necessary to rise in a modern bureaucracy.

Deep down, producers feel that anyone with rank or administrative authority has compromised his enforcement ethics to "get to the top." They see themselves as the "real police"— the "enforcers" who are willing to sacrifice friendships and advancement to preserve order on our streets. Of course, the word "willing" is misleading. The personalities of these officers generally render them incapable of any but the most blunt and literal interpretations of their function. But supervisors leave them alone because they do, after all, "produce." If a sergeant has one such man in his squad, he need not worry about filling squad quotas in the various statistical categories because his producer will carry the whole squad. However, he *will* find that the producer will come to feel put-upon and isolated within the squad, and will become a real thorn in the sergeant's side with his constant carping about the "laziness" of his colleagues. And the sergeant will always have to be concerned lest the man's poor judgment in interpersonal situations lands him (and thus his sergeant) in the middle of some touchy public relations problem.

The producer handles all his routine calls for service (that's part of the job), but more than most other officers he regards them as "horseshit" matters that waste his time. He hates (more than others) calming marital disputes and neighborhood quarrels, or dealing with the countless "petty" things which people so often feel merit police attention. He likes decisive interventions, such as clearing corners (where there is an anti-loitering law), making arrests, and issuing traffic tickets. He exercises discretion, but denies it by restructuring situations in terms of flagrant violations of law. For him "disorderly conduct" is not a relative, descriptive term but a precise description of whatever conduct he considers to be disorderly!

Because we have yet to come to grips with the realities of discretionary police authority (which is the producer's largest problem), the producer's main troubles are in the area of relations with colleagues. He does not regard his colleagues as real enforcers, and they regard him as an enforcement freak. They are well acquainted with his outlook, because it is the official outlook of the department and thus has been rejected or discarded along the way as inadequate to meet the needs of working police officers. They see the producer as a harasser of the public who enjoys the use of power in "chickenshit" situations. This does not imply that producers are afraid or cowardly. It merely states that they lack the ability to discriminate between situations that demand the ready exercise of power and those that demand a more low-key approach. If a producer consistently "backs up" other units on hazardous calls, and if he shows a willingness to get involved in fights where a colleague's safety is in question, he will be redeemed in the eyes of his nonproducing coworkers. Though they will still not like him, they will respect him and leave him to his idiosyncratic pursuits.

It happened to be a boring night, and the rookie, who wanted to get a cup of coffee, sit in a corner of a parking lot, and watch the world go by, happened to be riding with a senior officer, or producer. The senior man had cheerily decided that on this particular night he was going to empty his "safety repair order" book, and he counted up the twenty or so orders left. They began their enforcement mission, and every car with a headlight or taillight out received a repair order. But there were not enough of these to keep up the pace, so the officer began issuing orders for vehicles on which the small light over the rear license plate was out. After a few hours of wrenching accelerations, pursuits, and stops, he had emptied his repair order book and was thumbing through his moving violation citations to see how many of them he had left. His younger partner had a throbbing headache and was thus only partially thankful when the driver of the red Plymouth making an illegal turn turned out to be under age and in possession of alcohol. The traffic enforcement spree was over as they returned to the station to process the juvenile custody papers and call the boy's parents.

All officers have to "produce," of course, but producers make a parody of the concept. They approach their work with a sense of self-righteousness that transforms legal violations of civic authority into personal affronts to the officer's own sense of morality. When they issue a speeding ticket, for instance, the atmosphere is one of pursuit and revenge. The simple issuance of a citation takes on overtones of moral condemnation, as if the speeder in his violation represented all the disrespect for law and order in the community.

It is thus obvious that a handful of producers in a police district (and there are usually just a handful) constitute an enormous threat to positive community relations. Their contacts with citizens are numerous, brief, and negative. They lack "common sense" in their enforcement decisions because they do not share in the consensus of what is important and unimportant in effective patrolling. The contamination of professional decisions with personal and often rigid standards renders producers less able than other officers to distinguish degrees of severity in criminal violations. The traffic violator may therefore receive a verbal harangue more befitting an arsonist, while an arsonist may well fear for his safety and welcome the more predictable unpleasantries of the lock-up.

I obviously feel that producers are generally ineffective and sometimes dangerous police officers. I also feel that there is a lot of emotional immaturity, maladjustment, and even pathology in this group. The idea of the "producer" therefore subsumes more than a simple style of collecting a lot of patrol statistics. For these men, "statistics" represent a concretization of a vague and discretionary job and a source of feedback that they are doing their job well. The department rewards them, the courts usually must back them, and the public hates them. In this case, the discretionary powers that the officer wields have an essentially aggressive character, and the statistics accumulated as a by-product of this aggression toward the public become, in circular fashion, evidence that even greater aggressivity is needed.

In the long run, this style of patrolling produces more ill will and public alienation than anything else. It is regrettable that this style is not discouraged in an official way from within the profession. It certainly is discouraged at the street level by working officers, but these men are often under the same departmental pressures to "produce." Thus it is mainly the good judgment of most officers that cushions the effects of producers and softens their overall impact on the community.

The "crime fighter" represents a third style of policing. Like the producer, the crime fighter is not very philosophical about his job. Most of his thinking does not concern goals, values, or other abstractions, but rather specific tactical maneuvers to reduce the crime rate and apprehend criminals. The crime fighter will have definite ideas about the deployment of manpower, the use of plainclothesmen, and the like. He will aggressively develop informants. He will seek out and collect pictures of known criminals. He is always in more or less active pursuit of the "big arrest" (a felon) and resents having to spend his time on automobile accidents, dog bites, disorderly juveniles, vandalism, and other minor and service-oriented calls.

If anyone conforms to the standard TV image of the policeman, it is the crime fighter. He is enthusiastic about the pursuit of crime. He enjoys it. And generally he will take more than the usual risks to "get his man." Because he comes to regard patrol work as largely a waste of effort, he will often seek promotion or transfer to plainclothes or detective units.

If he succeeds in becoming a detective, he is the happiest man in the department, at least for a few years. He is free to devote all his time to the mission of fighting crime, and can work in a very independent manner to accomplish his goals. His speech, gestures, and attitudes take on that "cool," efficient, slick tone characteristic of movie and television detectives.

To a great extent the crime fighter is able to substitute enthusiasm for aggression. He experiences the conflicts and hostilities inherent in patrolling not so much as raw emotion but as a sort of sterilized "force" or power that can be fed into his private equations. His attitude is similar to that of the military tactician who thinks in terms of accomplishing the mission, pitting force against force and finding satisfaction in outmaneuvering, outthinking, outplanning, and defeating the opposition.

The crime fighter is not a hypercerebrate intellectual. He is not cold, nor is he necessarily that objective in his assessments. The key to his attitude lies in the transformation of complex human disruptions into a sort of large-scale urban chess game. There are, in his mind, three primary groups of people—those who enforce the law, those who break the law, and those who watch the drama. "The public" is experienced as an audience, and this lends an air of self-consciousness and importance to the crime fighter. Sometimes this air of importance is maintained even in situations of a trivial nature (e.g., "interrogating" a group of small boys caught breaking windows).

The process of investigation and arrest is conducted in a curiously value-free atmosphere in which moral judgments of the violator are often absent where one would expect to see them. Sometimes an unusually good rapport will develop between crime fighter and criminal, since each often perceives the other as a qualitatively different sort of power which must be respected if it is to be outwitted. This rapport, however, is a shallow one since the crime fighter suspends his value judgments only for the sake of the mission and always feels morally and intellectually superior to the criminal. This shallowness leads crime fighters to develop manipulative and deceitful ways of handling criminal investigations, and many police will admit that it was their own shortsightedness (not wrongdoing) that brought on the wave of Miranda-type Supreme Court decisions protective of arrestees' rights.

Over the long haul, such an adaptation can deaden sensitivities, increase cynicism, and produce a crime fighter who characterologically resembles more and more the criminal he is supposed to be fighting. This is more likely to occur in detective work than in patrol work, however, since patrol work tends in ironic fashion to shield the officer from the more frustrating aspects of our trial and sentencing procedures.

But while he is in patrol, the crime fighter will appear eternally restless, itching to do a job for which he has neither the time nor the resources. Because he is concerned with his image (remember that he sees himself as the embodiment of the movie-hero type), but does not have the detective credentials to go along with his desired image, he will generally compensate by being as "professional" as he can in his policing. He will be self-controlled, restrained, polite, and solicitous. The old-style cop will embarrass him because the image clashes with his own self-concept and reminds him of his present low status in the department and in the public's eye. "Professionalism" is an important word to the crime fighter. He is drawn to the status associated with the word, and sees himself in the vanguard of a new generation of law enforcement officials who earn the admiration and respect of the citizenry by their college educations, high salaries (hopefully), knowledge of the law, "coolness" under pressure, and aloof courtesy.

The crime fighter does not see patrol work as synonymous with police work. Patrol work is for those who lack the aptitudes or instincts for police work, i.e., fighting crime. But the crime fighter keeps this opinion pretty much to himself. He is sensitive enough to understand that advancement in a bureaucracy means alienating as few people as possible, so he makes a temporary peace with his colleagues while he tries hard to get himself promoted or transferred out of his predicament.[4]

Police departments love crime fighters. They represent all that is desirable to the current generation of administrators. They want a man who speaks fluently, clearly, and grammatically on the witness stand. They want states' attorneys and judges to read impeccable reports written in measured bureaucratese by their own officers. They want college graduates. They want men who sincerely believe in the validity and viability of their mission and who have the ambition to advance in the department, which means they are not likely to rock any boats along the way.

An officer does not have to have all the qualities mentioned above in order to be a crime fighter. He can be an old-style officer who develops informants and uses them to make big arrests. He can speak ungrammatical, even gutter, English, and can have all the suave professionalism of a peanut vendor. But he is a rare individual for the following reason: there is really no great reward for the crime fighter apart from promotion within the department.[5] The patrolman who, because of his education, mannerisms, or borderline legal tactics, does not fit the image of the new police professional is not likely to be promoted. New standardized civil service tests insure that one's ability to read, write, and memorize is at least as important as one's ability to fight crime in getting promoted to detective or to higher ranks within patrol work. A patrol officer who cannot score high enough on these tests looks around and sees others getting the same pay as himself without putting forth the effort that he does in his crime fighting activity. There is no incentive for him to go out of his way, and go out of his way he must if he is to develop a successful string of informants amidst the incessant stream of service and non-criminal matters that fill his days. Furthermore, he will find himself in a lop-sided competition with detective units working on the same cases, and these men will not be bogged down in service calls as he is.

The competition between patrol and detective units is legendary and legendarily one-sided. The resentment of patrol officers at detectives who "steal the show" is typified in remarks such as the following at a major crime scene: "Well, we all can go back to work now. The stars (detectives) are here."[6]

A young officer had been transferred about eight months earlier to the detective unit investigating auto thefts. He had recently written a letter to the captain of his old patrol district complaining about the poor quality of the stolen auto reports being turned in by his former colleagues. He urged them to describe in greater detail the colors and identifying characteristics of stolen cars so that they might be more easily identified by investigative units. The captain gave the letter to the old-time shift lieutenant, who then read it at roll call to his men. The lieutenant over-dramatized the reading of the young detective's flawless language, and he was interrupted gleefully and often by hoots and wisecracks from his audience. The men resented the efforts of the detective to make them work harder, and the lieutenant decided to take the opportunity to develop rapport with his men at the young man's expense. He commented, "Ralworth wasn't much of a policeman when he was out here, and I guess he isn't much of a policeman now either."

As crime fighters achieve positions of authority and leadership in police departments (and this they will do), the "old-timers" will find themselves under intense pressure to shape up or ship out. Detective Ralworth will one day have the last laugh, for better or worse.

No one will incur the wrath of the risen crime fighter more than the man who follows a fourth style of policing—avoidance. Avoiders go out of their way to evade work. They are unlike "safe" officers who do not avoid work but merely refuse to seek it out.

Avoiders, like all police, must perform a lowest common denominator of work. They must bring in at least a few traffic tickets a month (though they will always be below average, and proud of it). They must make at least a few business checks (enough to keep merchants from complaining), and they must respond to all calls for service they receive (what they do when they get there is another story). They must do their job, even with the sergeant's occasional prodding, or they simply will not last. But it is their conscious intent, from the beginning of the work day to its end, to do as little work as possible. If they are not answering a call, they will not fill the time by patrolling their post but will find a nice quiet place to hide. They will sit in a movie theater, or in the rear of a restaurant. Or they will watch television in a bar. They will back up other officers only on very hazardous calls, not because they are afraid, but because they have made a very sincere commitment to themselves not to raise one finger unnecessarily while on the job.

Every officer will at times avoid work, even if it involves

a simple maneuver such as leaving a scene where a dog is loose on a street. They do not want to get stuck with an "on-view" injured dog call that would take up an hour of their time waiting for the filthy truck from the municipal animal shelter, which passes for an ambulance, to arrive. And at shift change a good deal of avoidance goes on. Getting caught up in a traffic accident, burglary, or other felony here means that one gets home an hour late or worse. And no officer wants to work more than his "straight eight" hours unless he needs the overtime pay (which does not even *start* until he has put in at least one hour of overtime; in other words, the first hour is worked for no pay). Tactics here are complicated and numerous. One such tactic is to "stretch out" the time it takes to handle a call one receives in the last hour of the shift so that one is "out of service" for the remainder of the shift. In this way, any calls that come over the radio will be assigned to another unit. Officers who put themselves back in service as soon as possible after every call receive the respect and gratitude of their colleagues, but if they occasionally do not take advantage of a situation (as all others do) they are considered a bit "stupid" as well.

Another tactic is to "hide" in a quiet place during the last hour of the shift so that the chances of being summoned by a citizen on the street are minimized. Officers will also steer clear of traffic violations and car stops in the last moments of the shift, because these situations frequently blossom out into more serious affairs such as stolen autos, drunk drivers, narcotics, or persons wanted on warrants who must be arrested and processed by the officer who stopped the vehicle and investigated its occupants.

The avoider does not like his job. The safe officer also does not like his job, but finds sufficient compensation in the security and stability of a civil service occupation. The avoider cannot be compensated enough for work that he strongly dislikes. He will constantly be looking for assignment to "quiet" posts or "gravy" jobs within the department, or he may leave police work altogether if he is young enough to take up another career. If he is older, he will count the days until retirement. In the meantime, both young and old will skillfully manipulate sick time, leave time, and vacation time to maximize the amount of time they spend away from their job.

These men are the most cynical and disenchanted of all. A few are lazy, plain and simple, and would not behave differently in any line of work. But most are not characterologically lazy. Their disaffection and unhappiness show in their "drag-ass" postures and in their bored, far-off expressions during roll call. They look perpetually ready to fall asleep, or, in brighter moments, they look alert for any sign that work is on the way and beat a hasty retreat. They have an unabatable mistrust and hostility toward police administrators "downtown," who are perceived as the sources of all the unwanted pressures these men experience. They ridicule "gung-ho" crime fighters. Their attitude toward the whole bureaucracy is not unlike that of men drafted to serve in the military, who feel so much at the mercy of forces beyond their control that almost any means of retaliation is acceptable. Persons in positions of authority are by definition worthy of suspicion if not hostility. Anyone who embraces the mission of the organization is considered a fool. Anyone who volunteered for the work must be nuts. Of course, these men volunteered for their jobs and must reconcile this fact with their work-avoidance attitudes. And so they continually "bitch" and complain that supervisors are harassing them, or that too much pressure is involved in the job. They can never be pleased, for acknowledging the fairness of a supervisor would deprive them of their scapegoat; they would have to face the fact that every day they voluntarily report for a job they despise. There are occasional alcoholics among this group, and much depression. There are really no on-the-job sources of pride or self-esteem for the work avoider.

Strange as it may seem, the avoider is not universally disliked by his colleagues. Crime fighters and producers have no time for him, of course, but other officers are surprisingly tolerant. They get irritated, and sometimes infuriated, by the tactics of avoiders (the work obviously falls on the non-avoiders), but they are well understood by other officers. It is not an exceptionally pleasant job, administrators *are* maddeningly out of touch at times, and avoidance is, after all, something all police officers engage in some of the time. Avoiders tap a source of discontent in other police and externalize a lot of moaning and groaning that others usually suppress. At the same time, anyone who would seriously criticize an avoider would appear to be "gung-ho" and most officers do not desire this reputation either.

The net result is that avoiders usually survive, helped along by sympathetic colleagues provided that they pull enough of the load so as not to be too burdensome to the other members of their squad.

The avoider's approach to radio calls is the lowest of low key. Because conflict resolution through arrest often leads to court appearances (off-duty as well as on-duty), the avoider tries to steer clear of arrest as a solution. Whenever possible, the avoider will also steer clear of the onerous task of report writing. Most major incidents (felonies, for example) require a written report, while other incidents, minor in nature, can be given an "oral code" over the radio. If an officer receives a call for a burglary of a house, for example, and upon investigation finds that a window in the door has been broken, he can "downgrade" the incident from burglary to vandalism, make out a short "miscellaneous incident" report, and get back to the task of work avoidance. Of course he must first make sure that nothing is missing from the house. If the owner reports nothing missing, and if there is no sign of forced entry (broken lock, or pry marks), the officer can assume (not always correctly) that no entrance was gained.

A form of self-reward used by many officers is exploited fully by avoiders. This is the practice of buying goods and services from dealers who discount for police officers. Most modern departments try to discourage this practice, which of course makes it all the more tempting to avoiders. These men express much indignation if they cannot get a free clutch job for their car, cut-rate paneling for their home, or fabulous discounts on TV repairs or snow tires. The great efforts expended often for only a few dollars saved imply motives other than the purely economic. It becomes a way of "beating the system," of making their work worth *something* to them, just as the producer accumulates statistics in an effort to create some tangible reward for his efforts. One author has observed this tendency as early as in the police academy among trainees.⁷ The dynamics here are different, though. Academy trainees are conscious of their new group identity and their inheritance of a police tradition. They want to participate in the subculture and demonstrate in whatever way they can that they will help out their buddies. At this stage of the game, suggesting a store where discounts are given to police is a way of helping out another officer as well as a sign that a trainee already knows some of the ropes.

An avoider can be a terrific burden on a supervisor. To begin with, much of an avoider's style is attitudinal. He gripes a lot and overtly expresses his disenchantment with the job. He makes a point of letting everyone know he thinks most of the work is a lot of "bullshit," and that he is performing it under duress. He thus represents a challenge to the sergeant's authority and to the morale of his squad. But a sergeant cannot easily penalize a man for his attitude alone, and it can be difficult to pin an avoider down on substantive issues. Avoiders know the system well. They know all the excuses (as does their sergeant), and can use them without batting an eyelid. Policing is an intricate but muddled function. If an avoider is found in a quiet corner of a park by his sergeant, he can say that he saw a suspicious person who ran into the woods and came down to survey the scene. If he is caught off his post, he can say that he was pursuing a suspicious vehicle, lost it, and was in the process of returning to his post when the sergeant happened upon him. If his sergeant calls for him over the radio to meet him, and he is not in a position to do so without revealing that he is where he is not supposed to be, he can simply refuse to answer, or garble his response and then claim that he did not understand his sergeant's message because of temporary radio difficulty. (No one listening to a police radio can understand half of the subtle communicating that goes on under the guise of "official" broadcasting.) Both sergeant and officer will know that these excuses are precisely that, but the sergeant can take no formal disciplinary action without proof that the officer's excuse is invalid. Now, if a sergeant *wants* to drive an avoider out of his squad or out of police work altogether, he can do so. There are countless techniques he can use to accomplish this. He can call for the officer to meet him at different locations during the shift, and thus stretch the credulity of any excuses beyond the break-ing point. He can give the man unpleasant or degrading assign-ments, or he can insist on letter-perfect reports. A man's physical appearance can always be criticized, and there are enough rules and regulations that a sergeant can legitimately "get on a man's back" until he will beg for a transfer or resign. No one, in the long run, beats a determined sergeant. There is a delicate bal-ance of give and take in the sergeant-patrolman relationship, and if either party upsets this balance, it is a sure bet who will come out the loser.[8]

In a sense, the avoider creates for himself the kind of supervisor he resents so much. If he is tolerably avoidant and does not get involved in any personality clash with his sergeant, he will often be carried along as a nice guy and a body who fills a personnel slot. But usually such men get bounced from one squad to another until they either resign, are fired, or settle into some departmental position where little is expected of them and they can count the days until their retirement. As a turnkey, supply man, or clerk (but by no means do all turnkeys, supply men, and clerks originate from the disenchanted ranks of patrol avoiders), he can spend his days free from many of the pres-sures that bear on his colleagues in patrol, and he can engage in the casual rumor-spreading and reminiscing characteristic of men overwhelmed by a system they could not afford to beat. He will have lost the respect but not the friendship of patrolmen, who know too much to fault an ordinary man for failing in extraordinary circumstances.

It is difficult to explain the existence of chronic avoiders in a police department. Their numbers are certainly few, though in large departments civil service tenure may make their re-moval problematic. Their whole style runs counter to what one would expect from a patrol officer. They resist supervision, have no apparent taste for aggressive patrol, and do not contribute much to police services in the community. Why even discuss them?

The answer lies in the development of avoiders and in the observation that almost all officers understand this style, even if they adopt it only partially or on certain occasions.

Unlike the safe officer, who did not really expect that much from his job, the avoider probably joined the department with high expectations—perhaps too high or unrealistic. I do not recall anyone in my academy class who had an avoiding style, and I find it difficult to imagine anyone with that sort of attitude being drawn to policing in the first place. Something happens over the course of the probationary months and the first few years on the street. Maybe the officer endures a divorce, or a broken engagement, or the loss of a former circle of friends. Maybe he does not get a desired assignment or promotion. Maybe there has been a death in the family, or some other crisis at home. Maybe he fails to experience the respect, authority, or excitement he felt would come his way. It is obvious that he feels let down or disappointed for some reason, and he chooses to blame his profession for the hurts he has suffered. Given his profession, his perception of events may not be entirely inaccurate.

The avoiding style develops, I think, largely as a response to stress and disappointment. The disappointment may or may not be the department's fault, but the officer sees it as the department's fault. The style itself masks some personal failure or difficulty and is, in essence, the aggression of patrol work surfacing as resistance to the work itself. "Passive-aggressive" is a psychological term used to describe this apparent paradox.

If a supervisor has the freedom, sensitivity, and opportunity, he might be able to salvage a good officer. By directing the officer to counseling, or offering it in some way himself, a supervisor can relieve some of the alienation of the avoider and make it more difficult for him to think that no one cares.

I remember one avoider in our district who was a burly nine-year veteran with a sharp wit and sharper tongue. Somehow, one felt that he had at one time been an excellent street cop. But now he was a perpetual griper and clown. He also drank too much, and was beginning to drink on the job at selected bars. One night the sergeant was off, and the usual OIC (Officer In Charge) was also off. The shift lieutenant, who was a very old but quick-thinking man, appointed this man to be in charge of his squad for that night. The responsibility changed him dramatically for that evening. He spent most of the shift actively supervising his brood—checking on them to

see if they needed help, reading their reports, making sure they
had eaten, and generally making sure that all was well. His
primary concern, understandably enough, was the welfare of his
squad, since he felt his own interests had been neglected for so
long. The next evening the regular sergeant returned, and he
slipped back into the avoiding pattern.

The answer to the problem is not promotion to a higher
rank for all avoiders. The answer is a humane analysis of a
man's situation followed by appropriate help. The above illus-
tration suggests that the situation is at once sadder and more
optimistic than one might think.

A common style of policing, particularly among younger
officers, is the "street cop" style. Street cops approach their
work with a sort of contained abandon. They drive like maniacs
to be the first to arrive at a hold-up scene. They enjoy viscerally
any chases or apprehensions, and are very conscious of their
reputations for courage and willingness to commit their bodies
to the defense of their colleagues. They are enthusiastic about
their work, not in the "mission-oriented" sense of the crime
fighter, but because it affords them opportunities for simple
pleasures associated with fast driving, physical prowess, earned
respect under fire, and taking charge of chaotic situations. They
do not like spending their time on routine calls for service, but
they thoroughly enjoy being in a position to call someone else's
problems "routine." They take great risks every day, and label-
ling some citizen's complaint as petty only highlights the dan-
gers and risks they so zestfully take. These officers are easily
bored and like police work precisely because it is unpredictable,
varied, and stimulating.

In their private lives they often do adventurous, "non-
conforming" things such as camping, trail-bike riding, scuba-
diving, and the like. They are not very contemplative or abstract. They are happiest when engaged in active, physical work.
They are aggressive on the street and make a higher proportion
of "quality" car stops and field interviews than other officers.
(The producer engages in these activities, too, but does not
derive any more pleasure from a quality car stop than he does
from a routine car stop. It is quantity, not quality, that prompts

his behavior.) It does not particularly bother street police to stop a man whom they regard as suspicious and detain him for the fifteen minutes or so necessary to run a "wanted" check on him over the radio. They are not especially sensitive to the feelings of others (or, for that matter, to their own feelings), not because they are malicious but because their active temperaments do not allow for such exquisiteness in interpersonal relationships.

A new officer received a call for a DOA (a dead body— "dead on arrival") in a neat section of well-kept rowhouses. When he arrived, he was greeted by a middle-aged woman who tearfully related that her eighty-nine-year-old mother had just passed away in the upstairs bedroom. The rookie looked in on the dead woman, who indeed seemed to have passed far away, and decided to call for his OIC. He had never handled a DOA call, could not remember what had been rattled off in an academy lecture several months earlier, and decided that he could not afford to make any errors on such a call. When the OIC arrived, the rookie introduced him as "Sergeant Halley" to Mrs. Sandworth, the daughter of the deceased. (His use of the title "sergeant" here was an act of courtesy and deference extended to the OIC to make him feel better about having to be bothered with a rookie who needed help.)

By this time the grandchildren and Mr. Sandworth had arrived, and the house was heavy with that need for protocol and delicacy which accompanies grief (the undertaker's art). The two officers and the Sandworths retreated to the kitchen where the family phone was used to contact the medical examiner and the ambulance. While waiting for the medical examiner to re-contact him at the Sandworths' number, the OIC instructed the rookie on the details of filling out the DOA report. As an embarrassed and chagrined rookie listened helplessly, OIC Halley told him to mention that "You arrived at 2903 Burnview where you met Mrs. So-and-so." (Mrs. Sandworth was sitting at the table listening.) "She told you that her mother, Mrs. So-and-so, appeared to be dead in the upstairs bedroom." And so on. The young officer was glad when the instruction was over, for the OIC had referred to Mrs. Sand-

worth several times within earshot as "Mrs. So-and-so" after
having been introduced to her personally, and had referred to
the deceased as "Mrs. So-and-so" as well.

Street cops are the bread and butter of any police department. They are the ones who need the stimulation of the street
so much that they will put up with low pay, rigid bureaucracies,
shift work, low occupational prestige, and hostility from the
public to keep their jobs. They do not like the work as much
as they need it. Many leave, only to return after being bored
to death by other lines of work. They set the "tone" of the
police subculture. They are primarily responsible for the ethic
of pride and courage that often comes across to observers as
adolescent bravado. Their conversations resemble those of
action-oriented men everywhere. There is much talk about fighting, much joking about the snafus of friends, and much ribbing
about sexual experiences, normal or otherwise. These men respect an administrator who "came up through the ranks" without losing touch with his roots. They have no time for an
"outsider" brought into the department for his administrative or
managerial skills. They have a disdain for and a mistrust of
"book learning" which has intensified in the face of departmental efforts to use education as a partial yardstick to gauge
a man's potential for effective policing.

They feel that administrators will not back them up in
tight spots, so they back each other up with an even greater
determination. And the alienation they feel from "the brass"
goes for "the public" as well. Yet there is a surface quality to
these feelings. They are certainly real, and genuinely felt. But
they are also easily overcome, perhaps because the action orientation of these men leaves them little inclination to brood over
discouraging events. When it comes time to sell tickets to a
football game to raise money for the police boys' club, these
officers will go all out. (Producers will also find this challenging, for reasons of their own.) They will in some instances sell
ten times their allotment without resenting the fact that there *is*
an allotment, or that they have to do this at all. Nor do they
seem to resent the pressure put on them by supervisors to sell
their quotas (supervisors too are under pressure, of course).
Their reactions to other pressures are similar. They bring in

their car stops, they make their business checks, they issue their traffic citations—all without any serious or lasting resentment of the strongly implied pressures to "produce." They accept their job with a surprising willingness to tolerate situations which, if examined deeply in any abstract sense, might infuriate a less willing or more contemplative officer.

Despite their axiomatic suspicion and mistrust of authorities within the department, they can often be won over by a single meaningful gesture.[9] They are, like men in most strictly hierarchical organizations, very respectful of rank, and their opposition always has a puffy, bravado quality to it. When a man boasts that he "really told some major where to get off," he probably merely failed to add the word "sir" to an otherwise polite comment. Of course, there is always the rare maverick who "just plain don't give a damn" and *will* tell a major where to get off. Provided that such a maverick has justification for his show of disrespect and is in other respects a good street cop, he will achieve some heroic proportions in the eyes of his colleagues, and the recitation of his defiances will provide many a laugh in the roll call room. (Such an officer may find that he gains his reputation at the price of several vacation days taken from him by departmental trial boards.) There will be not a small amount of Br'er Rabbit in this humor.

The ability of street cops to separate rank from the person who holds it is curious in light of their own fusion of personality as the authority to be obeyed. If a citizen refuses to cooperate or becomes belligerent, it is taken as a personal affront by the officer. He becomes angry in return, and makes a point of teaching the citizen in question that *he* is not to be so easily slighted. Street cops have delicate egos ("ego" in the popular sense). Machismo is easily wounded. "Being a man" means continually announcing that you are the boss. And, as usual, there are good reasons for this. Most of the people the officer deals with on the street are men. Many of these men have failed so badly as workers, fathers, husbands, and lovers that they are hypersensitive to any implication they are not "manly." In this respect they share the attitudes of street cops toward authority and power. If an officer were to shrug off an insult as so much petty disrespect for his uniform or his official role, his attitude would be interpreted by the insulter as cowardice or fear. The street cop is well-bred for his role. He shares many of the assumptions of the public at large about manhood and aggression. He meets the public on this level, and he makes sure he comes out on top.

The street cop style fits the described duties of urban patrol better than any other style. This type of officer will feel less alienated from the department and from his work because his adaptation conforms so readily to what is expected of him. He is rougher, cruder, less polished, and maybe less "professional-looking" than public relations officials in the department would like him to be. He may even insist on some small sign of individuality—long sideburns, cowboy boots, or an unusual belt buckle—to announce his independence and bravado, and his disdain for "Mickey Mouse" regulations. But everyone realizes that he is the lifeblood of the occupation, the essence of the traditional patrol model applied to the seamy undersides of our cities.

Every officer, in fact, no matter what his style or adaptation, has to have some elements of the street cop in him. If he does not actually enjoy aggressive patrol, he must nevertheless prove capable of such activity from time to time. If he does not respond reflexly to territorial or personal threats, he must nevertheless recognize them when they arise and respond as if they meant something to him. If he does not readily use his body and his weapons as tools of the trade, he must nevertheless force himself to do so in spite of any fears or reservations he may have about physical force. And if he does not subscribe to the blunt philosophy of street cops, he must often squelch his misgivings in front of these officers and carry out his duties as if he "believed."

Street cops are physical people. They are not particularly conflicted about pushing, shoving, or striking others if they feel the situation warrants such behavior. And after all, the streets of our cities often are, in human and environmental terms, ugly and violent places in which to work. Because of this, it is far from certain whether college-educated police officers are going to have a definitive advantage over non-college educated officers. If you like peace and quiet, and if you appreciate beauty and kindness, you will find precious little of it in the public places of America's cities. If you like to go off by yourself and think about life, your place in it, and where the world is going —if you are the meditative or thoughtful sort—policing America's cities will grate against your sensibilities and turn you a trifle sour on mankind's potential for happiness. But if you went to college to advance your career and increase your earning potential, you may well find a home in one of America's police departments. Your perspective on law enforcement is needed, as is your rational approach to the severe management and identity dilemmas facing modern police.

It is doubtful that anyone who went to college with the goal of learning about "life" and people, and their history and purpose, will be happy as a police officer. An initial feeling that one is so learning by chasing winos out of alleys and by listening to people's complaints will rapidly evaporate under the influence of routine and futility. And very complex racial and generational biases will develop that strongly challenge any tendency toward even-handedness one may have had prior to policing.[10]

Because brooding is generally not in the character of the street cop, he can slough off many of the uglinesses and aggravations that face a police officer.[11] The residues of conflict do not accumulate inside him as they accumulate in other officers. He releases his tensions directly upon their source (the aggravating citizen) or through hard, fast driving and loudly obscene characterizations of the source of his frustrations. Other police will hear him out and understand perfectly, and all will feel better.

There are exceptions to this. Older street cops grow a little mellow with age, and they tend to feel the ugliness and tension around them a little more than they did when they were younger. Because the orientation of these men remains primarily physical, their internal conflicts and depressions will frequently find bodily expression in ulcers, headaches, and high blood pressure. These conditions are aggravated by the consumption of much coffee and over-the-counter greasy food, and by the rhythm of the work itself. The pace of the work is very slow, but punctuated at unpredictable intervals by explosive bursts of activity. This causes strain on the heart, and leads to the building up of high levels of anticipatory tension in the face of the unpredictable.

Minor aches and pains of all sorts are experienced by many older officers. Usually these back, leg, or shoulder pains are related to a street fight, an auto accident, or some other work-related event. As such, they are firmly enough grounded in reality so that no one can accuse an officer of malingering. Avoiders will exploit these aches and pains to their limit in efforts to get financial compensation, early retirement with partial pay, or even just an occasional day off (imagine the fury of an avoider who gets seriously injured in the performance of despised duties!). Street cops generally will not consciously exploit these pains, so the injuries assume an after-the-fact "somatopsychic" quality which does not compromise the "tough it out" ethic of the street cop while it allows him to mellow his aggressiveness a bit.

Jim, a fortyish officer whose style was about 50 percent safe and 50 percent street cop, pulled into the parking lot of a small shopping center in a neighborhood that had "turned black" within the past four years. He brought his car around in the characteristic police style wherein the drivers' doors are next to one another and easy conversation can take place. He told the other officer, who had not seen him in several weeks, that he had been hospitalized with a back injury. A few months ago, while parked on the side of a main road at night, his cruiser had been struck hard in the rear by a drunk driver, and Jim's back had been wrenched by the impact. Jim looked gaunt now, and his face was lined and pale. He complained to his friend in the other cruiser that the pain was well-nigh unbearable, that it was making him impossible to live with, and that he and his wife were consequently having a hard time of it. The doctors had apparently cut off any further pain relievers to avoid addiction, and the police department was taking its usual slow time to consider his case for an early retirement with disability benefits. (Jim ran several beauty shops and a small trucking firm in addition to being a full-time police officer.) He looked at a group of teenagers walking by and followed them with his eyes for a block or so down the street. "You know," he said, "when I first came out here I'd chase these little niggers with a smile on my face. Yeah . . . ," he repeated almost incredulously, "with a *smile* on my face. But now . . . Jesus!" The other officer had little to say but nodded sympathetically. *He* was still chasing "them" with a smile on his face. The radio cracked and Jim received a call for a group of disorderly juveniles up the street. Someone listening over a police radio would have no idea that the voice answering "2183, 10-4" belonged to a man in severe pain, fed up by years of chasing adolescents, and very close to the breaking point.

As implied in this last anecdote, there are few "pure" examples of any one style of policing. Almost all officers share some of the outlook and attitudes of the street cop. Even crime fighters with their professional orientation must "pay their dues" on the street before going on to greater heights. Safe officers are not as aggressive as street cops in ordinary situations, but will take aggressive action in major situations such as hold-ups, shootings, and burglaries. Avoiders view all situations, whether major or minor, as unworthy of their skins, and they will stick their necks out only to help another officer in trouble. An "assist an officer" call will bring an immediate response at high speed from virtually all police. All officers fight crime to a certain extent, all play it safe to a degree, all avoid work sometimes, all must "produce" within certain limits, and all must sooner or later be able to measure up on the street if they are to make a career out of mediating human conflict.

CHAPTER 6

Notes on Prejudice: Policing the Ghetto

IN THIS CHAPTER, I would like to air some views on the issue of police-minority relations in American cities. I cannot speak for all officers, and I especially cannot speak for black officers or officers of other minority groups. Nor can I speak for the black citizens of our cities. I will discuss my own impressions, attitudes, and feelings, and those of officers whom I came to know well enough to be aware of their attitudes on this issue.

There is a long and dingy history of police-black antagonism in the United States. The Marxist view that police exist to protect the economic interests of the propertied classes from encroachment by the poor is a bit strident, but it often has a gut-level appeal to many poor blacks. They are the enslaved, and the police officer is "the Man" who keeps them in their place, be it the cotton fields of over a century ago or the ghettos of our modern cities. It is a commonly held tenet of much liberal thought that police are brutal and fascistic in nature, and must be restrained and weakened at every possible opportunity in order to safeguard democracy and individual freedom. People accustomed to a more or less democratic form of government usually have at least some negative feelings toward the concept of "police." But blacks have a history that casts police in a definitively bad role. Police, especially white police, are the uniformed, visible embodiment of bigotry and repression. They are the cruel muscles moved by the mind of the larger bigoted society. They are, in every sense of the words, "the enemy in our streets."[1]

History and tradition are ongoing processes into which individuals are placed, to make their minor alterations or conformations as they will. The history of police-black relations in this country is such that alterations are extremely difficult. The upshot of this is that a rookie, white officer on patrol in a black neighborhood, be it lower or middle class, finds himself at worst in an atmosphere of pure hatred and anger, and at best in one of guarded mistrust and resentment. After enough leers, insults, obscenities, saliva globules, and bottles are tossed his way, he begins to respond in kind.[2] He cannot be too overt in his response, for if he responded quid pro quo, citizens would complain and he would be subject to disciplinary action. And on a more lofty level, his oath of office binds him to a standard of behavior inconsistent with any reciprocal abuse on the street. Some officers specifically request to work the poorest black neighborhoods because here the likelihood of anyone complaining (or of the complaint being taken seriously) is small, and these officers, often highly prejudiced over and above what the work alone would account for, can voice their racial feelings in relative safety.

Joe, a footman in a black ghetto area who himself lived in a small, white working-class enclave in the inner city, approached the group of five or six black teenage boys who were "signifying" on the corner in front of the carry-out. To "signify" means to act in a defiant, out-going way in order to assert one's claim on a given area or just to assert one's presence. These youths were attempting to assert their claim on the sidewalk in front of the store, and were bouncing, crooning, and gyrating as Joe and his partner walked toward them. When they were about fifteen yards from the youths, Joe said to his partner in a loud voice, "Look at all those fuckin' banana eaters." When he got closer, he announced to the group, "There's enough niggers here to make a Tarzan movie!" As Joe grinned menacingly at his joke and twirled his nightstick, the youths did not have to be told. They walked away from the store, trying to salvage some respect by some barely inaudible protests about "motherfuckin' po-leese."

Generations of Joes have made for a set of assumptions about police behavior by young black males that a rookie disregards at his own peril. Politeness and leniency are signs of softness and fear. Any attempts to play social worker are exploited in full by youths, many of whom have grown up exploiting social workers and their agencies. The word "nigger" comes to have a very special meaning to a white urban police officer. Far from being the naughty word of polite (and overly guilty) white liberal families, it is a word that says it all about the frustrations of policing a black ghetto. It implies baseness, dirtiness, cruelty, inhumaneness, and worthlessness. It gets a lot of built-up tensions off an officer's chest, and the relief it brings in a string of violently anti-black epithets often disturbs him. Younger officers especially find the change that comes about in their racial attitudes difficult to square with what, in the proverbial cool clear light of morning, they know to be the complex reality of the situation.

The reality is that people differ widely in their attitudes, morals, and standards of behavior. There are good and less good people of all races. If it were possible to walk through any neighborhood, black, white, or otherwise, and knock on every door, one would probably find the same proportion of friendly to hostile faces everywhere. Given the current social system, some people might be more cautious initially, but this probably would not represent a serious obstacle to communication.[3] The point here is that all generalizations are risky, and one cannot put things in their proper perspective without a lot of patience, time, and objectivity. These resources are often at a premium in police work. If you consider that police generally are not prone to excessive philosophizing, that the demands on their time are great, and that the pressures and aggravation of the work erode their patience over an eight-hour shift, it becomes clear that a white officer forms his impressions of blacks on evidence that is highly personalized, emotionally charged, and often superficial. He looks at "their" neighborhoods and sees a greater amount of trash on the streets and in the yards. And

you cannot tell him that it is because of poor collection practices by the city.

The trash in the alleys of a certain ghetto neighborhood
had reached such proportions that passage of automobiles was
impossible, not to mention the health and safety hazards involved. Some citizens in the neighborhood complained to their
city councilman, and he arranged to have a small armada of
sanitation trucks come by and clear the alleys of the discarded
mattresses, appliances, and other debris. After several trips, the
alleys were relatively clean. Three days later, according to police
who worked the area, they were virtually impassable again, the
trash having returned to its former proportions.

The behavior of teenage black males does more to prejudice an officer against blacks than any other factor. (It is interesting that older blacks rant and rave about the "kids," while
police rant and rave about "niggers.") Their speech, their mannerisms, their music, their gross concerns with pride and machismo (street cops are especially attuned to this), their defiant
attitudes, and their seeming proclivity for violent crime eventually turn the most well-intentioned officer against them.[4] He just
cannot avoid drawing some conclusions when virtually every
read-out at roll call involves a suspect who is a "colored male,
age 15-19." In the officer's mind, a statistically valid equation
forms between young black males and crime. And he sees too
much of the damage, in human and environmental terms, that
these youths cause to adopt a benign view of the situation.

After the daily litany of crimes and suspect-descriptions
had been recited at roll call, an officer in the last row turned to
his neighbor and said, "He sure gets around, doesn't he?"
"Who's that?" the other responded. "That 'colored male.' "

It has been pointed out that police usually overestimate the
amount of hostility felt toward them in the black community.[5]
After all, blacks are the victims of "colored male" far more frequently than any other group, and they have the most to gain
by an improved police response. But these authors (perhaps
because of limitations inherent in their questionnaire-oriented
techniques) miss the quality of the desire by blacks for more
and better police. It is not necessarily a desire for more friendly
relations with police, nor does it contain any sympathy for the

officer's position. It is a clear *demand* for a lowered crime rate and a safer community.[6] They want the police to do their job, they demand that the police do their job, and if "the job" (whatever that may be—perhaps the creation of a crime-free community, a task clearly beyond the capabilities of police) *is* done, the police will receive little thanks. The black community will simply be getting its long-delayed and just desserts.

Blacks more than any other group, I think, are prone to regard crime as somehow the result of police inefficiency or ineptitude rather than the result of a myriad of social and personal conditions. By putting the burden of solution on a government agency (a pattern set in the early 1960s), they avoid any personal association with the problems in their communities, and they preserve their basic belief in the integrity of "the people"—the valued democratic tradition. In their view, it is not the people who are at fault but government agencies, traditionally hostile and indifferent to the black community anyway.

It probably sounded like a fine idea. The Third World Art Society was going to have a block party for the people in the neighborhood on Memorial Day. They arranged with the city to have the necessary streets blocked off, brought in some old Ping-Pong tables, rented some ponies for pony rides, and set up the stereo and speakers. For several hours the mostly teen and pre-teen crowd had a good time. But toward the end of the party, the dance contest was continually interrupted by the Third World Art Society's moderator who could not keep enough order to continue the contest. Everyone wanted the floor at the same time. And the "Kung Fu" demonstration of the so-called "martial arts" was so mobbed that the demonstrators could not finish their routine. And there were so many kids climbing on roofs to get a better view that the whole proceeding had to be delayed for twenty minutes in a futile effort to get the kids off the roofs. The block party finished with a small mob scene of over one hundred teens and pre-teens running down the street and surrounding the half-dozen or so fist fights that were developing.

When the police broke up the crowd (no arrests were attempted) and dispersed the kids along several different routes, they received a call for a disorderly person back at the Third

World Art Society's building. A girl who had paid one dollar
to enter the defunct dance contest and who thought she had
won was attempting to collect, with the aid of her massively-
built father, the $50 prize money. The father was trembling with
rage as the Society representative explained to him that the
contest could not be finished because the crowd was too disorderly, and therefore there was no winner. He shouted for his
daughter's dollar to be returned. When the representative put a
dollar in an envelope, he demanded that the dollar be removed
from the envelope and placed directly in his hand. It was, and
he left. When the block party had finally fizzled to its messy
conclusion, an officer shook his head at the pathetic effort. "No
matter how hard they try," he muttered, "they *always* fuck
it up."

The black community has been a scapegoat for so long
that I am afraid the technique has been learned rather well.
How tempting it is to look elsewhere (e.g., to the effects of
discrimination or poverty) for an explanation of why the block
party could not be carried to a peaceful finish. And how difficult it is to acknowledge that, for whatever reasons, the neighborhood is more of a predatory jungle than a cooperative community. Identification with the Third World not only asserts
one's independence from a purportedly fascistic capitalism, but
also offers a form of fantasy-escape from the bleak and sordid
realities of ghetto life in America.

A new insurance company had opened up on a corner of a
main street in a poor black neighborhood. It was a one-man
operation, and the footman decided to make a "business check"
and meet the new owner before going on his lunch break. As
he walked in, the man rose, greeted him, and introduced himself as Mr. Howard. He was young, black, conservatively-
dressed, and apparently well-educated. He has some strong
ideas about revitalizing the black business community, although
he himself had just rented an apartment well outside the city,
much less the ghetto, limits. As Mr. Howard and the officer
stood in the doorway looking out on the street, they discussed
the city's failure to provide enough trash cans for the street,
thereby forcing people to litter. The frustrations of city politics
and bureaucracies were considered, as a few people discarded

crushed cigarette packs and candy wrappers on the sidewalk next to the one existing city can. The discussion was interesting and stimulating, at least for the officer, and both men seemed to be enjoying the "talk break." At that point Jimmy Brown rounded the corner and offered a loud, laughing greeting for Mr. Howard. Mr. Howard was in the process of getting acquainted with the people in the neighborhood and had met Mr. Brown the previous day. Mr. Brown made some joking comment about the officer's presence ("Hey, man, you ain't gonna lock me up, huh? Huh? HaHaaa! Yeah, baby!") and then lodged into a discussion of the relative merits of fucking fat or skinny women. Mr. Howard found himself a reluctant but brave partner to the discussion, much of which was unintelligible to the white officer. The crucial point apparently hinged on Mr. Brown's contention that a fat woman's clitoris ("cock" is the current anatomical street-word for this organ) is difficult to locate, whereas "if you show me a skinny woman, I know just what I'm doin'!" When Mr. Brown finally left, the nature of their prior discussion was so far afield of the reality of a slender woman's sexual organs that Mr. Howard and the officer said goodbye and went back to their own businesses.

A fundamental factor in the development of police attitudes toward poor blacks is the dominance of concrete sense impressions over more abstract, "intellectualized" reasoning. The impressions made on an officer by rats, filth, noise, screaming, blood, vomit, burned pork lard, roaches, wrecked housing, and human feces on his shoes will rarely be outweighed by any factual information concerning the emerging black middle class or the results of an opinion survey in the black community. Yet real prejudice is not as rampant among police as many often assume.[7] The truly prejudiced officer literally "pre-judges" people solely on the basis of race. He makes very few allowances for individual differences, and decides that a person is a "nigger" just by seeing his skin. Most officers realize that their feelings are just that—feelings—and they can ill afford to base their judgments or actions on feelings alone.[8] You cannot fault a man for his gut reactions. These are elemental reactions that he cannot really control. He can only be faulted if he makes these reactions the basis for his behavior on the job—if he affords people less than the best of his judgment because of Pavlovian associations unavoidably collected in the course of his daily work.

By the same token, an officer is often forced to judge people on the basis of superficial cues. The nature of his job allows little alternative. He simply does not have time to look "beneath the surface" of a person to find the "true self." He infers that self from what he sees, hears, and senses on the surface. Skin color alone is a superficial cue with very little predictive value for an officer. A person's skin color tells him little about how that person thinks, feels, or behaves. (The same is now true for long hair on white males. It became so prevalent that it lost whatever predictive value it may have had.) But many blacks, particularly young, poor blacks, exhibit more superficial cues than do others, perhaps because they are more concerned with "signifying" and making some concrete imprint on their surroundings. Flashy clothes, sunglasses worn in the dead of night, or a self-conscious strutting tell an officer that a person "has an attitude." He is likely to be so concerned with proving his own worth and defending some small shreds of pride that he will become obnoxious if approached in any but a polite and rational manner. (Even this will be resented, which is why most patrol officers seem rather gruff and insensitive to observers. The consequences of polite and impolite—short of downright insulting—behavior by police are the same: they end up being resented and despised.)[9]

The expression on a man's face can tell an officer a great deal. Many black males look as though they are continually hurt or angry. In teenagers these feelings find expression in a "pout." The head is turned slightly upwards and to one side, and the corners of the mouth are drawn down.[10] A few more years of futility and hopelessness turn their boyish insecurity into a rather inflammatory rage, often directed in shotgun fashion against the world at large. In extreme cases of deprivation, young men begin to look cold and bland. They look at you without making any human contact. They are grossly insensitive and can be gratuitously vicious. Their lives represent the distillation of all that is poisonous in the current urban climate. They are detached from meaningful human relationships, and their detached contact with a police officer can be deceptively calm. It is the vacant, yet powerful iciness in their eyes rather than any more overt acting-out that indicates they are dangerous. And I cannot help but wonder whether this look is actually respected and dignified among certain circles as the essence of "coolness" and "badness." I *do* believe it speaks volumes that the word "bad" now means "good" in the jargon of inner city youths.

Black women generally do not represent much of a problem to police, as long as they are not crossed or thwarted too severely. Most black women, it seems to me, are not nearly as submissive as the women a white officer might be used to. They can give an officer the hardest time of his life if he is unfortunate enough to impose himself where he is not wanted. An officer usually develops a healthy respect for the tradition of maternal dominance in poor black families, and is generally thankful that these women have better things to do than roam the streets in search of their cultural identities. Black women are also more skillful at "using" the police to serve their own ends than are other groups in society (politicians aside). A white woman who is being beaten by her drunken husband will, for example, call the police and state exactly what is happening. The police will respond with their usual reluctance to get involved in an inevitably messy and problematic marital dispute. However, a black woman in the same situation will call the police and exclaim that there is a "man with a gun" or a "man with a knife" in her house. This will bring an immediate response from several police at the same time, not because they do not know that they are party to manipulations but because they cannot afford to take a chance that the situation is not what it appears to be.[11]

It was about two o'clock in the morning. The station wagon went slowly through the red light in a middle-class, racially-mixed area. The officer pulled out of his secluded spot and brought the vehicle to the curb, looking more for a car stop and a verbal warning at that hour of the night than a traffic ticket. As he approached the driver's window, a large, thirty-fivish black woman leaned out and glared directly into his eyes. "I suppose you stopped me for that red light back there," she bellowed. "Yes, ma'am, I did," he answered. "Well, listen here," she continued, her face drawn tight in indignation. "I've got a sick girl here in the back seat and I'm bringing her home from the hospital, and . . ." The officer looked at the girl lying on the back seat (who may or may not really have been sick) and interrupted the woman, whose righteous anger was rising. "OK, that's fine, go right ahead, no problem, that's OK." The woman had bristled with all the superficial cues the officer associated with categorical, maternal defensiveness. Given the minor nature of the violation, he could not let her go fast enough.

An officer also associates groups with trouble. A group of four or more young males (since we are discussing urban ghettos, we will say black males, while recognizing that young white males are also suspect, and with good cause) is suspect, no matter how they are dressed or how they are behaving. The officer knows from crime statistics and roll-call read-outs that the power of a group has special meaning to people whose individual power is negligible. He will generally follow such a group for a while to let them know he is watching, for he strongly suspects that they will end up committing some petty crime or act of vandalism. Of course he realizes also that they may be travelling in groups for their own protection. But even an elemental sense of contemporary history teaches that when everyone's advantage is equalized, the results of violence are all the more serious.

Perhaps the greatest single source of misunderstanding and bad feeling between white police and poor blacks is the enormity of the cultural differences between the two groups. It takes a white officer at least several months of constant exposure to ghetto life to understand the basic assumptions under which ghetto blacks live. And until he reaches that understanding (and often afterwards, too), the ghetto will be a strange, alien, and difficult place in which to work. Picture the following scene: It is 2:30 on a Saturday morning, and the last few party-goers are inching their way home in efforts to avoid drunk driving charges. The major six-lane road that runs through the ghetto neighborhood is virtually deserted. Cars are parked in the far left and right lanes, leaving two lanes open on each side of the

median strip. On one of these lanes a car is parked, with the
lights out and doors open, and eight people of varying ages and
sexes are inside and outside the car. Does this situation call for
police action or not? In a white neighborhood this would be
a rare situation, and an officer usually would not hesitate to
inquire as to what the people were doing parked in the middle
of the road. But this is not a rare situation in a poor black
neighborhood. Ghetto residents often stop their cars in the
middle of through roads to carry on brief conversations with
friends on the sidewalk, and the buildup of traffic behind them
seems only to strengthen their desire to "signify" their claim to
that section of the street. But at 2:30 A.M. they are not really
causing a traffic jam, and the advantage gained by clearing the
street would not offset the cacophony of protests and obscenities (and possible violence) that would greet any efforts to move
them. So an officer (unless he has adopted a very aggressive
"street cop" style of patrolling) takes a cursory glance to insure
that no one is holding a gun at anyone else's head, and leaves
well enough alone.

Aggression and cruelty hang over the ghetto like an in-
fectious smog. Small boys carry sticks around with which they
beat and torment the dogs that many people have penned in
their back yards as protection against intruders. The animals
are often mangy, underfed, lame, covered with welts and scars,
and half-crazed from living in cramped, filthy quarters. They
are at the bottom of the pecking order in the ghetto, just a
notch below children. The children occasionally spur two dogs
on to a fight in much the same fashion as "sporting men" of
years ago arranged cockfights. Virtually every boy over ten is
armed with some sort of weapon, be it a knife, a thick stick, a
small handgun, or some miscellaneous tool.

As the older officer and the rookie climbed the small stoop
to enter the corner drugstore, a group of boys in their early
teens was leaving. As they passed, the older officer spun around
and jabbed at one boy's rear pants pocket with his nightstick.
He flipped the nightstick up, and a shiny object sprung into the
air as the boy fled down the street. The rookie retrieved the
object and wondered at the older officer's perception and his
adroitness with his stick. It proved to be an umbrella handle

with about six inches of the metal pole sticking out of it. The boy had broken the pole off to leave an ugly, jagged point at the tip of his makeshift knife. The rookie was to come across several of these in the next few months.

A ghetto is a violent, predatory place, especially for the people who have to live there. An elderly black person can count on a mugging or a pursesnatch as surely as he or she counts on Labor Day or Christmas. Youngsters who avoid gangs or street crime are persecuted and taunted for their weakness by those who do not avoid these activities. Children grow up in an environment of filth, fear, and fighting, and an officer often has occasion to marvel at the charm and friendliness these children manage to show toward him. Everytime he passes a group of small children he is greeted with a chirping chorus of "Hi, Mister Po-leese" or "Hi, Officer Friendly."[12] He has equal occasion to regret the fact that these children have to grow up.

The events of the past ten years make policing a ghetto a very dangerous task as well. Crime has become, to a great extent, politicized. Shooting a police officer has become a semi-revolutionary act with overtones of liberation and pride in one's heritage. The potential for violence is great in these areas, and it does not take much to trigger its release. People who have little to lose are always dangerous. People who, with whatever justification, are hypersensitive to any encroachment on their free will or their self-governance, are extremely problematic from a police point of view. The law is, after all, a rather clumsy tool, and it is clumsiest where it is used the most—in the ghetto. Loitering laws are a good example. Cities and police departments have found through experience that the invisible "boundaries" that separate shops from sidewalks and sidewalks from streets do not seem to apply to a ghetto area. Bar patrons spill over onto the sidewalk as if there were no such thing as a door to separate "in" from "out."[13] Because of this, large groups would gather outside bar entrances and make passage along the sidewalk, or in and out of the bar, difficult. Bar owners complained that their business was suffering, that minors were being given alcohol, and that the small crowds frequently became unruly and disruptive. It became necessary to pass city ordinances to the effect that no one can stand within fifty feet of the entrance to an establishment that sells liquor. Since standing is not necessarily loitering ("I'm waiting for the bus, officer"), and since many grocery stores and carry-outs sell liquor, considerable discretion is involved in the enforcement of anti-loitering laws. Suppose an officer sees two men carrying on a quiet conversation on the sidewalk in front of a bar. He decides that no cause is served by telling these peaceable gentlemen to move on, so he walks by. Others see him take no (apparent) notice of the men "loitering" in front of the bar, and the next time he comes around there are a few more on the sidewalk to test him. If he walks silently by this time, he will be faced with an even larger crowd on the next trip, and he *will* have difficulty moving them. They will argue and protest, figuring that the officer is lenient, green, or afraid. The net result is that two men's pride must be insulted by a clumsy application of law in order to ward off larger problems that will ensue if the law is applied more discriminately. In this case, the officer's discretion is limited by citizen perception of his behavior.

This "corner clearing" ritual is as ludicrous as it may be necessary. It is axiomatic that a group will gather on any sidewalk where there is a bar. When they see a footman coming they move inside, and when he is gone they return to the sidewalk. When he comes around again, they move inside again, and return to the sidewalk when he leaves. They will not disperse at the approach of a patrol car because too many cruisers pass them with better things to do. A cruiser will have to stop, and the officer may actually have to leave his car and impose his body on the scene at close range to countermand their claim to the sidewalk. But an officer in a car does not have to get involved in the game-playing one-upmanship of "corner clearing." He may be on a call, so the sidewalk people do not draw any negative inferences concerning his courage or toughness from the fact that he fails to assert his claim on their territory. But the footman has no such "out." As futile and ridiculous as it is, corner clearing has definite meaning to the parties involved. The footman who clears the sidewalks is as despised as the footman who does not. Only the reasons differ.

It often seems that the principal means of persuasion in the ghetto is fear. The ability to inspire fear is a respected quality in an officer. He need not be physically large, but he must have the primitive and vulgar capacity to meet the challenges of predation on their own terms. His gun means a great deal, to himself and to the people he polices. If they ever suspected that he was afraid to use it, or afraid to use his nightstick, they would take full advantage of him. ("They" here refers to those ghetto residents who live on, or supplement their incomes with, the fruits of others' labors, or who have become so desensitized to cruelty that violence becomes merely a form of stimulation in a boring environment.) There is also a primitive strength in numbers, which police rely on fully as much as do juvenile gang members. Through his radio an officer can summon a small army to his aid, often in a matter of seconds. The strength of the police is vast, and sometimes seems to be their only respected quality in the inner city.

If one is diplomatic enough to avoid provoking people unnecessarily beyond the point where fear restrains anger, and if one is reasonably alert and cautious, policing a ghetto is not as dangerous as is commonly assumed. But it is definitely upsetting work. One learns to fear one's own impulses to aggress as much as those of the citizens who prompt these retaliatory feelings.

It may have become apparent by now that the assumptions and characteristics of police and policed in a ghetto become rather similar. This is felt acutely by some police, who either accept their lot as "niggers of the working world" in a resigned fashion or actively contrive to exaggerate the differences that exist between themselves and the "niggers" of society.

It was a bleak, cold, and rainy night in mid-February. Toward the end of the shift, the old sergeant had picked up the footman and was letting him warm himself in the patrol car before walking the last hour. They were parked in a recess behind a gas station and could see an occasional person hurrying by on his way home. "Man!" exclaimed the sergeant, "there ain't nothin' out there tonight but niggers. And rats," he added, as a soaked vermin darted about the trash cans in search of home. "Yeah," muttered the thawing footman. "The niggers, the rats, and the police."

When young officers are urged by their elders to be tactful, restrained, and self-controlled, the warning is always put in the following terms: "Don't bring yourself down to their level. If they want to act like animals, that's their business. But don't put yourself on their level. If you do, you're no better than they are." One officer had recently purchased a small foreign car and was thinking of selling it to purchase a large, American-made sedan. Since it was the middle of the gasoline crunch (February 1974), I asked him why the switch? "Look at these niggers," he replied. "They've all got big cars, and if they can have big cars then I can have a big car too." The showy materialism and ostentation that many whites see in blacks have a firm hold on them as well. A white officer coming from a working-class background (as so many do) has an antipathy for poor blacks that only empathy could nurture. He holds on to his property and to his hard-earned signs of success with a tenacity that is beginning to make itself felt in such issues as school busing and public housing development. Blacks represent economic and social chaos to the lower-middle-class white. If blacks move into his neighborhood (and it will be *his* neighborhood they move into), the value of his property will decline. The crime in his neighborhood will increase. And the general quality of life in his area will, in his estimation, decline rapidly. At best he will be surrounded by neighbors who, in today's racial climate, will be as distant and aloof from him as he is from them. And yet, with some exceptions, he cannot be dismissed out of hand as an incorrigible bigot. He will acknowledge that most blacks are probably as desirous as he is of a peaceful, settled community. But someone will have to explain to him why, whenever a neighborhood "changes," for some inexplicable reason the crime goes up, the quality of schooling goes down, fear becomes the dominant community feeling, and trash begins to collect in alleys and on lawns and sidewalks. He does not understand, so he fears and resists. And he can become quite ugly about it. If he is a police officer, he finds very little in his daily work to ease the anxieties engendered at home about the future of his home and his children's schooling.

The conflict in a conscientious officer between his emotional reactions to blacks and his better judgment is a conflict that rarely finds final resolution. An officer, no matter how negatively he might feel toward "blacks" (a general group-focused term), will almost always deal with each individual case on its own merits.¹⁴ And if he ends up being harder on blacks than he would be on whites who commit the same offense, it will usually be due to the fact that an antagonistic or hostile attitude is demonstrated openly toward him more often by blacks than by whites. Here we are not dealing so much with racial as with attitudinal behaviors, racial only insofar as an officer might find them more often among blacks than among whites. But he will always be torn between the simplistic satisfactions of a vengeful racism and the demand, created by his job, that he keep a fairly open mind and be ready to modify any conceptions he forms about a person based on their outward appearances or mannerisms. Occasionally this conflict can make him feel very bad indeed.

Two officers were standing by the entrance to a city incinerator on a hot July night. The sanitation workers were on strike, and the officers were detailed to monitor the picket line that was blocking the incinerator entrance. Four pickets had been arrested earlier in the day, but by 9:30 in the evening things had settled down to the point where police and sanitation workers were sharing coffee, Cokes, and conversation. The entrance to the incinerator was immediately off a major and well-trafficked truck route, and the dust and smog created by all types of vehicles passing within inches of police and pickets alike were uniting them in a feeling of shared discomfort. In addition, police had just rejected a contract with the city and were in labor troubles similar to those of the sanitation pickets. The net result was a feeling by police not of camaraderie or of sympathy, but of simple respect for working men trying to get a better deal for a hard day's work. There was none of the contrived conviviality which every "liberal" white has experienced in the company of blacks. The police monitoring the picket line did not even say goodbye when their shift ended. All understood that when an unpleasant job is finished, one thinks only of home, a shower, a cold drink, and some familial affection.

On that same evening at that same picket line, a black boy about eleven years old rode up on his bicycle and stopped to talk to a policeman. He had been living with his aunt and

cousins, but they had treated him so badly (refusing to feed
him adequately and making him perform an inordinate amount
of work around the house) that he had decided to return to his
"real mother's" house on the other side of town. He had run
away from his aunt's place on his bicycle and had pedaled
nearly forty miles in hot, noisy, and dangerous truck traffic
before deciding that he could pedal no farther. As he asked
the officer for a ride to his mother's place, tears came to his
eyes, and he sat down exhausted next to a telephone pole to
rest. One of the sanitation workers overheard the boy's problem
and volunteered to have one of the picket replacements ride
him home. An officer gave him a quarter for a soda at a gas
station next door, and while he awaited the arrival of his ride,
another officer talked with him about the intolerable conditions
at his aunt's house. The boy talked about the times he had been
picked up by the police for glue-sniffing even though he hadn't
sniffed anything and claimed that he didn't even know what
glue was. "What *is* glue?" he asked. The officer was a bit skep-
tical, but he recalled his own experiences with glue—expensive
model airplanes and elaborate projects in a small, private elementary school—and gave the boy the benefit of the doubt.
The boy also told how he wanted to be a fireman (he followed
the fire engines in his neighborhood on their calls, and was
thrilled one day when a firefighter's boot fell off a moving truck
and he was able to retrieve it and toss it back), and how one
of his neighbors got shot by the police (he didn't know why,
except that the man was "running way"). After about half an
hour his ride came. The bike was loaded into the trunk, and
an eleven-year-old boy with a lot of guts and eleven-year-old
dreams rode off to face an uncertain welcome at his "real
mother's place" in one of the roughest parts of town. The officer was left with his typical mixed feelings about his reactions
to blacks. He regretted all the times he had dismissed a black
kid as a purse snatcher or a bike thief simply because he had
neither the time nor the inclination to get to know him better.
He regretted all the times he had judged a black man as dirty
or stupid, when he was really returning dead-tired from a day's
grind on the back of a city sanitation truck. He regretted that
his own job made such little allowance for the complexity of

an individual, and that major decisions often had to be made on "surface" predictors alone because there was no time or opportunity to put things in their proper perspective. At the same time, he felt anger toward the cruelty and callousness of the boy's aunt and cousins. He knew this cruelty well. It was the same blunt viciousness and insensitivity that raised welts and sores on the back and haunches of almost every ghetto dog he had ever seen. It was an insensitivity that at times did not distinguish between a dog and a small boy with dreams who had not learned what glue is.

CHAPTER 7

Notes to Social Scientists, Especially Psychologists

AT A 1974 convention of the American Psychological Association, I had occasion to sit in on one of four colloquia devoted to the work psychologists do with police departments. Two things seemed to stand out in all discussions of this area. First, psychologists are becoming more and more involved with police departments, particularly major metropolitan departments. Second, almost all psychologists experience considerable difficulty in establishing solid, or even barely workable, relations with street patrolmen.

If these two points seem contradictory, let me resolve the discrepancy this way. Psychologists generally work with the administrative levels of police departments (e.g., recruit testing and screening, education and training of recruits in human relations, application of management principles). In police departments, as in no other organizations in America (at least to the same extent), there is an incredible gap between administrators and "line" personnel that is virtually impossible to bridge. Administrators, as we have noted in Chapter 2, spend much of their efforts trying to attain impossible goals so that the present unrealistic equilibrium of police fictions held by police and public alike will not be disturbed. One of these impossible goals is the thorough supervision of line personnel. Because policemen are individualists who work alone according to their own styles and preferred patterns of patrol, and because they must handle a variety of difficult assignments often with no formal supervision, police administrators have long relied on fear, or the threat of disciplinary action, to keep their line "in line." And yet the police behavior to be regulated in this fashion usually has nothing to do with the work of the patrolmen per se. It is concerned with intradepartmental procedures and regulations. Administrators apparently feel that if they cannot regulate substantive police behavior (and they usually cannot), they can at least regulate procedural behavior and hope that traits of obedience thus established transfer to the substantive sphere as well.

Administrators are openly frustrated by this arrangement, and line officers are openly contemptuous of it. They interpret their situation to be "the real" one, and regard administrators as out of touch with the reality of street policing. Hence the oft-heard feeling among patrolmen that "Nelson was a good cop in this district, but then he went downtown (got promoted) and those oak leaves went to his head" (gold leaves being the insignia of a high rank in this department).

Coupled with an acquired suspiciousness of "outsiders," a distrust of non-police, a lack of interest in "book-learning," and an antipathy for "bleeding hearts," there is another particularly bothersome obstacle that policemen present to someone who attempts to bridge the administrative-line gap. This is the fiction of paramilitary organization. To a certain extent, the paramilitary structure of police departments is an inheritance of the past and survives, in part, because it has built up a "head of steam" through the years. (At the same time, the oldest metropolitan police department in the country is only about 150 years old.) But the paramilitary organization is also designed to afford the appearance of strict discipline and obedience of orders by subordinates—a goal we have seen is actually impossible to attain.

People unfamiliar with the realities of police work (as most of us are) often assume that policies and beliefs held by a top administrator will filter down to the street level and will be picked up by line officers, much as a general's order will be obeyed down the line by all subordinates. In police work this simply does not happen. A social scientist who consults to management levels of police departments will have no lasting effect unless he follows through and makes contact with the men on the street. In fact (although this may be my own bias), were it possible to bypass high command levels altogether, more meaningful and lasting results could be obtained.[1] But this is wishful thinking. No one gets any work with police done without first obtaining the approval of top officials in the department. The mistake is not working with high officials but failing to work through them to the street level, where any change of any kind is either going to be manifested or sabotaged.

Administrators know this, and they know that they themselves can short-circuit change by insuring that consultants have no contact with line officers. Modern police departments have a peculiarly contradictory quality that makes the work of consultants very difficult. Since most metropolitan departments want to appear "modern" and "professional," they feel constrained to do modern and professional things like hiring consultants from outside agencies to study current problems and make recommendations. Yet the personnel occupying high-ranking positions within these departments came up through the ranks during years when policing was so intertwined with organized crime and machine politics that only the frailest pretense could be made that police were seriously trying to further some development other than their own personal finances. What I am saying is that it is very likely that police departments hire consultants as much to say that they have done so as to work toward any substantive development of the police craft. Thus, it is not an infrequent experience for a consultant to enter a police department and realize months later that he is doing something quite apart from the job for which he was hired.

Police are experts at bureaucratic manipulation and pressuring. They are acutely attuned to power games and power struggles. They are cynical about using power and influence, and they are masters at doing so in quiet, almost imperceptible ways. A rookie's first month in a new precinct is a crash course in non-verbal, exquisitely subtle, pressuring, hint-dropping, quiet manipulation. If he does not catch on, he will not make the grade. If he does catch on well, he may make chief one day.

Any social scientist who cannot, for seemingly puzzling reasons, gain contact with line officers should become suspect of the motives of those who hired him. And any social scientist who is content in his role without contacting line officers (unless his job is exclusively management-oriented) should wonder whether he is being seduced by high-ranking officials who shake his hand enthusiastically and tell him how valuable he has been to "the department."

One of the problems psychologists have in working with police is that they are generally not grounded in basic social research on policing. Most of the descriptions and analyses of policing have been done by sociologists, and it was an historian, Jonathan Rubinstein, who in his book *City Police*[2] gave us the most thorough, honest, and expertly researched description of the police craft to date. Psychologists should be familiar with such works. It would prevent a lot of confusion and ill feeling when they sit down and "talk shop" with a street cop. Also, psychologists should involve themselves more in this type of basic descriptive research. The traditional psychological research paradigm is, admittedly, ill-suited for this sort of work because it calls for rather tightly controlled conditions, reasonably accurate "measures," and some tangible results, usually in the form of statistical representations of complex variable relations. Much has come out of this paradigm that can be, and has proved to be, of use to police. But a harmful side-effect has resulted as well. Because most of the research is done outside police departments while the results are applied within police departments, psychologists have never picked up an intuitive grasp of police the way they pick up knowledge of other groups (e.g., military groups, students, personnel directors, hospital staffs, advertising executives) for whom they consult. There are notable exceptions (Dr. Robert Shellow of Carnegie-Mellon University, for example) who demonstrate that psychologists can make meaningful and productive contacts with police officers. The conditions under which police and psychologists can get together are unique, however, just as the conditions are unique for any group. That they are not widely understood does not mean that they cannot be achieved if understanding takes place.

For example, one psychologist in the colloquium felt that were he to ride in a patrol car with police, they would "test" him in ways that would put him in morally untenable positions. If they took a free meal, for instance, he would be constrained to take a free meal too, and would be deeply conflicted about the moral implications of his complicity. A proper understanding of the meaning of free food and other gratuities might ease this psychologist's mind. As Rubinstein points out,[3] the issue of gratuities is best seen not in the light of morality, but in light of the complex system of reciprocal services and relationships that exist between city dwellers. Let us suppose that police in a district regularly visit one doughnut shop during their shift because the manager gives them free coffee. The street police see nothing wrong with this arrangement. They give the store a little extra attention, and in return they get free coffee—quid pro quo. However, if there is another doughnut shop down the street that receives little or no attention because the manager insists that police pay for their coffee, the question can be raised as to the propriety of police conduct. Is it fair that one store be penalized because it chooses not to engage in a quid pro quo arrangement with the police? Note here that the individual act of taking free coffee from one shop has no moral relevance to the patrolman, to the store manager, or to anyone else directly involved in this informal and reciprocal arrangement. Morality is an alien issue, imposed from without by someone who does not understand the complex of collusions that evolve among city people dealing in services to the public. The issue relevant to the police task is the effect such collusions have on the allocation of police resources, and whether any such effect renders them more effective or ineffective as a result. The question is not "Should I or shouldn't I take this coffee?" but "Will taking this coffee involve me in a relationship with this establishment that will compromise the quality of my work?"

There is another feeling among social scientists that would present little problem if properly understood. This is the feeling that policemen simply do not trust "outsiders," and have a reflexive rejection of anyone who does not fit into their group. The social scientist who believes this either steers clear of police altogether, contents himself with contacting only administrators, or winds up co-opted into the police subculture, convincing police that social scientists have nothing substantive of their own to offer and are really ineffectual fellows after all.

While police *are* often mistrustful of those with whom they do not work, it is not often understood that even other policemen are often considered "outsiders." A policeman who, regardless of how much "time" he has on the force, is transferred to another district will be considered an "outsider." He will meet with the same perfunctory courtesy and caution as will a visiting social scientist, although the commonality of shared working assumptions will facilitate his acceptance considerably. Any rookie is considered an "outsider," often until his second year in the same squad. Policemen from the same district but on different shifts will not develop the closeness that develops between members of the same squad. Some detectives are treated coolly, along with high administrators and others deeply steeped in the police subculture.

The point is that police do not have some unique, dichotomous system of classifying people into "outsiders" and "insiders." The extent to which police accept other police more easily than they accept non-police is a function not so much of group affiliation as of shared respect and loyalty. It is not often the patrolmen meets someone who has his best interests at heart. It is not often he meets someone who genuinely wants to ease his burden and understand the difficulties of his job. It is not often that people willingly and whole-heartedly "back him up," offering support and sympathy (both physical and emotional) in tough situations. Most non-police who try to become friendly with police are "police buffs," whom police instantly recognize as having motivations other than the genuine wish to understand and help. They like the toughness, or the power, of police. They want special favors, or their brother is a policeman, or they used to be policemen themselves, or they want the vicarious thrill of the high-speed chase or the shootout. Or, as with some social scientists, they want merely to succeed at communicating with what others consider to be a hostile, pariah group—"status slumming," as it were.

The motivations of the social scientist need not be purely altruistic. Police would not believe such a thing exists anyway! But he must be honest, and he must, apart from whatever financial or career gain he expects out of his efforts, be primarily interested in helping to make the patrolman's job an easier one. As Dr. Shellow noted, this will often strike home with police officers, whose job is made more and more difficult as years go by.

The social scientist must also abandon any conceptions he has that he is "the expert" at human behavior whose job it is to critique and modify the decisions made by patrolmen on the street. Expert he may well be, but he must not forget that police officers are experts at human behavior as well. They will resent and resist anyone who, because of academically acquired credentials, purports to know more than they do about people. It is axiomatic in police work that the officer's decisions are not openly criticized, especially in front of other police. If a sergeant wants to thoroughly humiliate an officer, he will criticize the man's decisions in front of his colleagues or (the ultimate degradation) in front of citizens. But he very rarely does this, even to a rookie, because the implications are so gravely negative for the unfortunate man in question.

The problem for the social scientist here is not one of substance but of etiquette. The question is not "Do I have anything to offer the police in the way of advice?" but "How can I best communicate my ideas to the police given their strong belief in the autonomy and finality of individual decisions?" The answer is—carefully. The best approach here is to draw out the considerable stores of knowledge police hold but rarely, if ever, verbalize. If, for example, a police officer yells at a group of juveniles standing on a corner to disperse (because there is a loitering law, or curfew, or some other reason), and they curse and taunt him until he finally has to drive up to the corner and leave his patrol car before they scatter, the social scientist can remark that "Those kids seemed like a worse bunch than the other kids in the district." This will involve the officer in a dis-

cussion of the juvenile problem in the district and tune him in
to comparing these kids with other kids. The observer can then
say, for instance, "It seemed like they were a real pain in the
ass to move off that corner. Christ, you had to get out of the
car and everything!" On hearing this, the officer may well come
to his own conclusion that yelling at the kids from a distance
was a mistake, and that imposing one's body at close range is
often required to move people from their preferred territory.
This, of course, is the observer's criticism. But he has avoided
being judgmental toward the officer and, in fact, has purposefully
placed the blame for the incident on the juveniles so as not to
make the officer defensive. What he has done (which no other
police "critic" ever does) is provide the kind of curious "I
wonder why" sort of atmosphere in which the officer can discuss the incident, drawing on his own experience to externalize
and make explicit a fact about interpersonal distance and
corner-clearing. And of course, the observer has learned something from the officer about the juvenile problem in the district
and about the importance of local territories as stages for
clashes between police and juveniles.

If the police perceive an observer as someone who is going
to give them expert advice on how to do their job, they will
often "set him up" to look like an incompetent. They will give
him "What would you do if you walked into a bar and . . ."
examples which, being in the province of the police art and involving such things as force and physical coercion about which
the observer may know nothing, have no rote answer. If the observer has no answer, he should say so, or even better, acknowledge the skill of the police in these areas ("What would I do?
I think I'd call the cops!"). Police will give you enough rope
to tie a noose and hang yourself if you are so inclined. However,
there is no need to be ingratiating. One must simply confess
ignorance where ignorance exists, defer to police judgment in
their areas of specialty, and follow the etiquette of not criticiz-
ing or challenging the decisions or styles of the man who has
extended to you the privilege of sharing his working world.

No matter what the task of the consultant, he will be successful only if he respects the skill of police. His job should be
one of facilitator, of one-who-helps-to-make-explicit, of one

who asks darn good questions that cause police to verbalize their large stores of intuitive knowledge about interpersonal behavior. He must also respect the relationships that exist in the department prior to his arrival and that will exist long after he is gone. This includes relationships police have with merchants, local neighborhood figures, other police, waitresses, firemen, and the like. But the most important man the social scientist must deal with is the sergeant of the men he wants to work with. The men will be waiting to see what Sarge thinks of you, and if Sarge says "thumbs down," you will get nowhere. The relationship that exists between a sergeant and his men is incredibly intimate and intimately reciprocal. The sergeant is charged with supervising a group of men who differ in terms of their styles, temperaments, and conceptions of what police work should be. They work autonomously, and depend on him to protect them from administrative harassment and to allow them the autonomy which, by departmental regulation, he should not give them. He in turn depends on them to bring in the expected numbers of car stops, arrests, parking tickets, and so on, which they could curtail considerably were he to harass them or insult their autonomy as individual workers. He depends on them not to "let him down" by getting caught in violation of regulations (the sergeant is also penalized according to the fiction of paramilitary supervision). The men do not say they work for the police department, or for the public, or for their captain or lieutenant. They work for "the Sarge." He is their only real boss, and even if they do not like him, his good graces must be maintained by conforming to his demands and expectations.

Thus, if a social scientist can also get in Sarge's good graces, he will have closed much more than half the distance to a good working relationship with line officers. The sergeant is supreme in his squad, and a social scientist should approach him with all the deference, cordiality, and respect that were afforded the police chief when he first contacted the department. In many respects, this is the most important man in the department. His control over his men is absolute (or rather, his conviction that he alone *should* control his men is absolute). He guards his squad like a mother hen guards her chicks, and will be as defensive and attuned to encroachment upon his brood. He will be afraid that the delicate balance he has (hopefully) established between conformity and autonomy among his men will be upset. He must be assured that it will not be. He may be afraid that the inevitable foibles of his men will somehow be exposed by a researcher and will leave him wide open for censure or embarrassment. Because he is more involved in power struggles than his men (due to his rank), he may be naturally more suspicious of a researcher's (or a consultant's) motives.

The sergeant must be assured and reassured. Explain your interests and your goals. Spend a good deal of time explaining exactly how you came to *his* squad, whom you talked to "downtown," what you heard, where you come from, under what auspices, what is to become of your presence in his squad, of your work with his men. His need to know who pulled what strings to land you in his domain must be satisfied or he simply will not trust you. And do not be in a hurry to leave him and get to "the men." Spend all the time he wants you to spend with him. If you have explained your purpose, he will know you want to be with his men, and he will allow that when he sees fit. (You will not get anywhere without his approval anyway, so there is no hurry!)

A more subjective judgment may or may not be correct, and may or may not be reassuring to social scientists interested in working with police departments. It is my own feeling that the temperamental and interpersonal-style differences between police officers (as a group) and social scientists (as a group) tend to be large. (Political, attitudinal, educational, class, and other gross differences are well documented.) Even considering that there are many "false" misunderstandings between the two groups, based on reciprocal stereotyping and mistaken assumptions, it is not true that police are simply social scientists whose working world takes the edge off their basically humanitarian impulses. The differences between police and social scientists have been implicit in much of what has already been said in this book about the "police personality." The disinclination toward abstract thinking, the action orientation, the social conventionality, and the desire for a "real, down-to-earth" view of things are some of the points at which a social scientist might find himself aground in dealing with police.

The key to effective consulting, or observing, is thus an ability to suspend (temporarily) some of one's habitual ways of relating to others and of conceptualizing one's environs without becoming co-opted into a framework that is essentially alien to one's own values and experiences. Actually, if one is not too heavily invested in one's own phenomenological perspective, the adoption of another person's point of view need not be all that problematic. However, I have met countless social workers, psychologists, and academicians who simply could not (nor should they) feel at all comfortable in the presence of police officers who are wrestling a vomiting drunk into a paddy wagon. Nor could they expand (or would it be narrowing?) their perspective to accommodate the patrolman who waits near a stop sign at the bottom of a hill to "get his statistics" for the month. If a person is embarrassed, put off, repelled, or shocked by force, by rough humor, or by what appears often to be plain interpersonal insensitivity, he may well be in much the same position as any newcomer to the entrails of America's cities, including many rookie policemen. However, if he fails to gain some insight into the realities of policing and if he finds himself totally unable to empathize with those who do the policing, he may well question whether police work is a viable area for his professional activity.

Psychologists should be especially careful about their personal feelings when it comes to the issue of training police officers. All too often we approach policing as if it were "beneath" us, as if the role of consultant presupposes an expertise in the specifics of patrol work. We tend, then, to regard policing as a perfectly obvious activity, and we airily formulate training procedures and goals infused with our own values of egalitarianism, group sensitivity, and intellectualism. From where we sit it seems easy to construct training models for police. But we are setting our own trap if we fail to gain what experienced professionals feel is essential to successful consulting with police—first-hand patrol experience (i.e., riding in a radio car for several shifts).[4]

Because we often do not want or are prevented from getting such experience, we are often trapped. Our human relations seminars, our sensitivity training sessions, our packaged movie and cassette gimmicks, and our various personality theories and sociologies fall on deaf and hostile ears. We then come to retaliatory and hurtful conclusions that police are indeed rigid, close-minded, and incapable of transcending their own pasts. They are, in other words, untrainable. A particularly unfair conclusion goes something like this: "Further, more intensive and more concentrated training is needed." This, however, only passes the buck and sets a nastier trap for the unfortunate consultant who follows. It suggests an attitude of hopelessness and futility. It also implies the more covert assumption that training police is fundamentally an attack phenomenon—a process wherein the forces of science and rationality mount an assault on the forces of backwardness and dogmatism.

I would venture the perhaps extreme opinion that social science has oversold itself—to police and to others. We have no "magic answers," and our analyses, however accurate, often lead to no clear remediation or recommendations. We fell into the vacuum created when sophisticated police technology pulled ahead of personnel and training practices. We thought we could bridge the gap by stuffing it with expertise derived from other fields, notably industrial and organizational psychology, personality research, and sensitivity training. So in many departments officers came in off a hard and grubby night of unpleasantries and read memoranda ordering them to report to the Education and Training Division the following week for a class on Human Relations. Failure, resistance, and hostility were guaranteed by the compulsory and condescending nature of the training and, admittedly in many cases, by a rather determined and negative attitude toward anything having to do with a book or a classroom.

I do not wish to blame consultants or police for the current inadequacies in police training. To a great extent, no one is to blame. But were I to point the finger at anyone, I would find it hard to avoid the high-level police administrator. For he has, in true paramilitary fashion, imagined that one can order a man to learn as simply as one can order him to drive around the block. He has assumed that placing an instructor in the same room with a group of "students" constitutes a sufficient condition for the occurrence of education. And he has, in his unimaginative approach to the whole concept of selection and training, betrayed a grudging attitude toward flexible and modern practices. That is why police continue to hold paramilitary rank and why they are suited up to look more like commandos on parade than enforcement officers serving the public interest.

It is up to police departments to upgrade the quality of their police, and it is up to social scientists to curb their greed, cultivate humility, and become more selective in what they are willing to do as consultants. It does no one any good to set everyone up for failure.

CHAPTER 8

Notes to Police:
An Editorial on Ethics

LIKE THE PRIEST discovered having an affair, the psychiatrist whose children are "problem kids," the professional football player who is gay, or the successful celebrity who commits suicide, the dishonest cop mystifies and disappoints the public. He confirms the worst suspicions of some and strains the faith and trust of others. It is often assumed that his authority and role carry with them a morality and ethical standard above reproach.

If this assumption of public trust is not rare among occupations, neither is it widespread. It seems, in fact, to be shared only by those in whose care people place their physical or emotional well-being, for whatever reason and for whatever length of time. Such jobs include doctor, airline pilot, nurse, and bus driver. (It is, of course, no accident that these occupations are usually associated with a uniform of some sort. The individual with all his idiosyncracies is de-emphasized in favor of the trusted role which he fills.)

The Watergate episode of recent years has highlighted the dynamics of public trust and occupational morality in a way that many of us have never seen before. The potential for disillusionment was so high during those months that it was not uncommon for people actually to become angry at the press and

135

other media for spelling out the facts of the case. But if stoning the bearer of bad tidings did not help, neither did recalling Teapot Dome or the myriad of scandals that have rocked other governments at other times. Every population has its own expectations of its leaders, and those expectations are not easily turned aside by historical analysis.

Repeated assaults on the public's investment of trust by those so entrusted cause anger, disillusionment, and outrage. Initially a period of denial may occur. But over time, the profession or group in question assumes a stereotype all its own, and this stereotype is usually negative and fairly resistant to change (e.g., the oft-maligned used car dealer). Major housecleanings open to public review and scrutiny are often the only way to demonstrate that the original investment can be recovered and invested once more. Hence we have the "openness' of the Carter administration, the divulgence of CIA and FBI data, the airing of all sorts of files and records formerly considered confidential, the beginnings of so-called "sunshine" laws, the adoption of "zero-base" budgeting, the declaration of officials' personal finances, the dogged (if clumsy) investigation of foreign influence-buying in the Congress, and competitive advertising by lawyers, to name just a few elements of our national reaction to official betrayal in the early 1970s.

The process of corruption and the public's reactions have important implications for the police community. Police are indeed "in trouble,"[1] though seen in historical perspective (for what that is worth in terms of public relations) the pendulum has swung nearly 180° from the dismal days of the early century.[2] Let us zero in on the meaning of this trouble, but first let us rule out a few topics.

Rule out, for instance, the flagrant instances of police immorality that appear not infrequently in almost every major newspaper—"Sheriff Operates Prostitution Ring," "Officer Sought in Assault on Youth," "Police Indicted in City Numbers Racket," and the like. There is no need to document, refute, deny, or belabor the wrongness of these things. To a great extent they are seen by the reading public as individual acts by men who succumb in the face of temptation. The profession as a whole does not depreciate as much as one might expect, and there is much awareness that news media highlight such stories for their catchy or paradoxical theme—the law enforcer breaking the law. Moreover, people usually discriminate among branches and types of law enforcement, so that the archtypal small-town Southern sheriff, for instance, is more likely than a Bureau of Customs inspector to abuse the public. Teenage gang members or others familiar with the police on a street level discriminate even more finely, and know which officers are "straight" and which are crooked, which are fair and which are unfair.

Let us rule out, then, any notion that "police corruption" is a unitary concept like "medical malpractice,"[3] and let us credit the public with a certain flexibility and intelligence when it comes to evaluating widely differing segments of the police profession. This should forestall our overreacting to instances of ethical violations and plunging headlong into unrealistic attempts at renovation. As an example of this sort of measure, I will quote from the "Law Enforcement Code of Ethics" adopted by an otherwise progressive department: "I will keep my private life unsullied as an example to all; maintain courageous calm in the face of danger, scorn, and ridicule; develop self-restraint; and be constantly mindful of the welfare of others."[4] This Code, in its entirety, is noble and earns high marks from the President's Commission on Law Enforcement and Administration of Justice as an ideal toward which to aim.

However—and I hope I am not just being picky here—it smacks of the Boy Scout Pledge, the POW Code of Conduct, or the Hippocratic Oath. That is, it is a gesture so unrealistic and general as to be useless as an ethical guide. I should also note that the Commission heaped lavish praise on J. Edgar Hoover, much of it deserved, for the transformation he brought about in the FBI. However, since the Report was printed, much has come to light concerning the operations of Hoover and the Bureau under his direction that cause one to reconsider such blanket praise. Let us further rule out, then, any hopes we might have that the fostering of paramilitary conformity or the recitation of oaths can effect ethical behavior in enforcement officials.

Let us, finally, try to track the discussion of police corruption away from issues of morality and into the sphere of professional ethics. What is the difference? The difference lies in the officer's—and in the public's—conception of responsibility. When an officer sees his occupational conduct in terms of morality vs. immorality, the distinction between his personal and professional standards is minimized. If one is a moral person, then one will be a "good" police officer, and if one is an immoral person, one's immorality will not be restrained by a badge and an oath of office. Just as the idea of authority can become personalized in police work, so too can the idea of morality. And when these things are personalized, their implications for colleagues and for the profession as a whole are correspondingly minimized or not recognized at all. The officer's sense of responsibility stops where his obligation to the profession begins, and he is not likely to see his individual acts, privately motivated, as reflecting significantly on the general esteem or reputation of his department.

So far the public has been fairly charitable, largely because our culture has chosen to fuse law and morality to a great extent, and to view the "corrupt" officer more as an individual sinner than as an incompetent professional. Moreover, until recent years, little was expected from police, and petty theft and graft were just a small part of a larger influence-peddling and corruptible political system. But as policing becomes less of a trade and more of a formalized profession, the yardstick of morality is going to fall short of providing a system for the evaluation of police responsibility. As the officer is given explicit discretionary power and the training and apprenticeship necessary for its judicious use, the "shoulds" and "should nots" of today are going to evolve into a sense of autonomy and self-direction, so that the occupational identity itself rather than a "Ten Commandments" code of conduct serves to guide the officer's conduct.

Take, for example, the overworked subject of accepting free meals. Police instructors in the academy say it over and over and over—if you take that free cup of coffee, you will soon graduate to doughnuts and coffee, then move on to sandwiches, sodas, snow tires, "Christmas gifts," and cash payments for extra protection. And soon thereafter you will be running errands for the Mafia, playing illegal numbers games, protecting drug traffickers, and even assaulting innocent citizens in your accelerating slide down the greasy tube of corruption.

I am making a caricature of this approach not because such progressions have never occurred (they have), but because like the gruesome films in driver training classes, an overblown description of the worst possible errors is not a lasting deterrent for those faced with many small errors. It is irrelevant to everyday functioning, and since it is based on fear, its effects are short-lived and easily forgotten. For example, consider the following unfortunate rookie just two weeks out of the academy.

His squad is assigned to picket duty during a strike by city school teachers. Five officers pile into a patrol car on a cold February morning and decide, as always, to stop for coffee and doughnuts to go. The new officer is sitting in front on the passenger side, so he is the logical one to take orders for cream and sugar, plain or filled, and so forth. When they pull into the doughnut shop, he thinks he has all the orders straight. But he turns to let the others know that he does not have enough change on him to pay for everything. He is told not to worry about it, that this store does not charge police. They go back to their conversations. The rookie feels trapped between his desire to be as ethical as possible and his need to learn the prevailing district mores, which include in this case a very relaxed and casual assumption of free food at this store. He does not have enough money to cover everything, and he cannot get any from his colleagues. He wants to respect these men, and basically he does. He will not believe that he is the only one in the car with any sense of right and wrong. His fellows just are not the corrupted ogres the academy warned against. He is reasonably sure that he is not being tested or used. His statement about not having the money already showed his attitude, but his attitude apparently does not make much sense or difference. So he goes into the shop, collects the order, and leaves a dollar tip for the counter girl. He is embarrassed and feels like a freeloader. He learns that when he is with other officers, he has to adapt and keep his alert system in order lest he go too far. He trusts his colleagues and likes them. That helps, but it does not wipe out the discomfort he feels over the whole business.

He recognizes immediately that he was ill-prepared for this minor situation, and decides that working alone is going to be a lot easier than working with others.

After several months on the street, I found that I was more comfortable with minor lapses of diligence that I had initially found disconcerting. This was particularly true when I worked with older officers whose fundamental integrity and good will were known throughout the district. I sloughed off most of that hypersensitivity to duty that every rookie brings with him, and settled into the difficult process of learning by myself just what was permissible, what was forbidden, and what was borderline in the real world of the district. At different times and under different circumstances, things such as dropping in on a movie for ten or fifteen minutes on a boring afternoon, accepting a discount meal, or running a personal errand (drycleaning, for example) while on duty could be anything from harmless to irresponsible. Consider, for instance, the consequences if an armed robbery should occur on the sidewalk outside the movie theater while the officer is inside cooling off or resting his eyes for a few minutes. Police learn to take chances. They learn to apply the laws of probability in a way that maximizes their chances of getting away with the small liberties they create for themselves. And, of course, they learn a thousand excuses for those infrequent times when their guesswork fails them.

To be honest, though, what bothered me most about these things was not any lofty idea of violating professional ethics, but the simple embarrassment of being so visible in one's laxity. People who saw us going into the movie theater knew we were not investigating any crime. People who had to pay for their food noticed our discount. People knew that we were parked in the shade to cool off and chat. (I recall one very embarrassing time when a small group of elderly ladies passed our parked cruiser and clucked their disapproval over my partner's loud snoring.) On these occasions I felt as though we were losing a lot of face—pride, if you will—and fueling already strong notions that cops are arrogant about the public's feelings and less than scrupulous in executing their duties. I felt in a poor position to command respect from the fellow next to me in the doughnut store forking over his money.

Another fallacy of academy training concerning corruption is that merchants are often out to corrupt police. This is just not true. Some are on very friendly terms with the regular beat officer, but this has to be put in context. The officer might use the employee restroom to wash up, or hang his raincoat in the back office, or leave his briefcase there while he walks his beat. Certainly the department has made no such provision for these small but necessary conveniences, so the officer works out what he can on his post. And if he can arrange to be around the store when the owner leaves to take the day's profits to the bank, who is to say that this reciprocity of courtesies is immoral or unethical? Any simplistic rule or regulation governing the mutual accommodations of merchants and police is going to be irrelevant and ignored. However, this is not to say that there is nothing wrong with the present state of affairs.

The problem here—and in most cases of professional laxity (let us use this term and save "corruption" for the major and rarer ethical violations)—is one shared with other occupations weighted with public trust. It is that the interactions and arrangements between the services and those serviced are so complex as to defy attempts at imposed regulation. The regulation must therefore come from within the officer, based on his own sense of the importance of his work and his judgment about what enhances or tarnishes the quality of that work. This sense involves three elements: pride, self-consciousness, and objectivity.

Pride in this case is a feeling that policing is a prestigious and valued responsibility involving considerable skills at a variety of tasks under frequently trying circumstances. Police often complain that the public does not perceive them this way. But they are less eager to point out that they themselves have developed rather crude and unarticulated conceptions of their work as unrewarding, grubby, low-paying, and a waste of time. They reduce their skills to a lowest common denominator of "common sense" and force, and thus occasionally lose sight of the larger meaning of their work. Their vision of how they fit into the complexities of the social system becomes myopic, and exists more to discern "friend" from "foe" than to evaluate the host of relationships in which they are entangled. I do not question their patrol judgment or their "sizing up" of people and situations. This they do and usually do well. I think, however, that they get bogged down in small tasks and concrete decisions, and lose a perspective on just why they are on the streets in the first place. I also think they have received precious little help from anywhere in preserving their pride, and that the role of the police officer in American culture is entirely too personalized and dependent on individual whim for its definition. Unfortunately, the vacuum left to individual whim is occasionally filled by other forces.

It is here that "political corruption" comes into play. In the absence of an independent and professional sense of dignity, police often allow themselves to be used by politicians or others influential in the community. I recall two personal instances of this happening.

The first involved a car that had been sighted speeding up a busy road and running a number of red lights on the way. I happened to pull the car over, and two other patrol cars pulled up behind me. When we questioned the driver, we found out that he was from "Eddy's Used Cars" and was taking this car somewhere for Eddy. When the other officers heard this, they put their notebooks away, gave him a verbal warning, and headed back to their patrol cars. However, I was not party to any knowledge about Eddy and besides, I was resigning from the department two weeks later and had little to lose by offending a minor politico. I gave the driver a ticket for running a red light, and he nonchalantly got back in his car. One of the other officers mentioned something to me about Eddy being a nice guy or a friend of the police, and I responded by telling him that I was resigning in two weeks anyway. Several weeks after I resigned, I read in the paper something (I can't remember the details) about Eddy's generosity to the local Democratic party. I never learned, nor at the time did I care to learn, why he liked police so much.

The second "political" experience I had involved my assignment with another officer to a foot post that had just been created in a lower-middle-class white neighborhood bordering black sections of the city. The post was supposed to be temporary, in response to some acute crime danger, and we reported to the home of a certain family on our first evening of patrol. I honestly do not know why we went there, but the man of the house was a friend of someone "downtown" who had talked to someone else who had contacted our district about this foot post. I was given no background information, but simply followed my senior partner's lead. I do not recall the "acute crime danger" ever being specified. We sat down in this man's living room and had a soda, then walked around an area of about four square blocks for the rest of the evening. We "knew," basically, that we had been assigned to walk around this man's house using enough extraneous territory to disguise the fact. His bathroom, telephone, and refrigerator were at our disposal. He was obviously not a wealthy man, but his connections had apparently been strong enough to get a "couple of cops" sent on a one-week goose chase. We never used his bathroom or his refrigerator, and my partner used his telephone once to call the sergeant. We did not think much of this guy or our assignment, but we did not question arrangements beyond our control.

The politically powerful tend to bask in each other's reflected glory and cover each other's tracks. So the ordinary patrol officer hardly ever realizes the sources of some policies and decisions that affect his work. If anyone believes that "you can't fight City Hall," it is the police officer. The days are gone, I think, when payoffs to ward leaders were necessary to join the police department. And civil service exams and merit systems have replaced policies of promotion-by-payment. In other words, most of the classic and blunt elements of politico-police corruption have been phased out. What remains is more subtle, is well-concealed, and is not very clear to many of those affected.

We should not underestimate the corrosive effects—the insulting effects—of political manipulation on the integrity of the enforcement process. Pride is essential for a functional sense of ethical conduct, and nothing destroys pride faster than a debasement that one cannot resist. If an example is necessary, witness the sad morale problems in the FBI following public disclosure that the Bureau had been used toward political ends outside its charter in the 1960s and early 1970s. And if it is to Mr. Hoover's credit that he resisted a good many Executive attempts at manipulation, it is to his discredit that his own political concerns assumed dimensions ultimately destructive of his own professional ideals.

Self-consciousness is a second supporter of ethical conduct, and it implies only that officers should be aware that people are watching what they do, that people care what they do, and that people want them to do a good job. It is stating the obvious to say that police know they are watched and evaluated by the public. But it is not so obvious to police officers that people wish, by and large, for ideal police who are strong, brave, and true—in short, all the qualities we see in our noble oaths of office. In the public's eye these are important qualities, despite their uselessness to officers in need of practical guides.

Understanding this sense of self-consciousness is easier if one thinks of other professions, or even of policing, as portrayed on television. Doctors are idealized as Marcus Welbys and Richard Kildares. Lawyers are vaulted to near sanctity as Perry Masons or Hannigans. And police come over as the admirable characters in Adam-12 or a host of other shows. No medical school or law school points to these examples as ideals, and police academies mention Adam-12 only in terms of its unrealism. But that is not the point. What must be kept in mind are the idealized expectations of the public, and the ideals of the fledgling members of these occupations. People want our professional skepticism and "reality" like they want a hole in the head. Every doctor who talks with a patient understands— no matter what the patient might say at the time—that the professional responsibility lies with him, that his own doubts can only harm his patient, and that while honoring the truth he must not destroy his patient's hopes in medical science.

An airline pilot would have similar feelings toward his passengers were his plane to develop serious engine trouble in mid-flight. There is simply nothing to be gained by crying one's woes in front of an audience that trusts and depends on one.

It is true that police take a lot of abuse from a relatively small section of the public. It is true that they may feel underappreciated and used. It is true that their pay and prestige are often below what they feel they deserve. They do not have the weight of the medical and legal traditions behind them. In fact, their tradition is anything but admirable in American cities. By the same token, they should keep in mind that until fairly recently, educated men avoided physicians like the plague itself because their methods (purges, leeches, bleedings, plasters, and the like) were so crude and unreliable as to actually harm patients. They should remember that airline pilots—a highly trusted and prestigious group—were known only a few decades ago as reckless and zany adventurers. And they should remember that when J. Edgar Hoover took over the FBI nearly fifty years ago, it was an operational and ethical wreck.

All of these professions matured by researching and perfecting their methods of operation, by modernizing their technologies, by emphasizing and demanding the strictest admission standards and training possible, and by having the self-discipline and self-consciousness to realize the importance of their idealized forms in the public mind. I see every reason to believe that policing can follow this now standard route to occupational dignity.

A third element determining high ethical standards is objectivity. By this I do not mean that one performs in robot-like fashion, or that one treats all human situations as though they were categories evoking some predetermined response. One cannot and should not remove personal feelings from one's work, especially when that work concerns other people's lives and emotions. One's own feelings are, in fact, a very powerful and useful tool if one learns how to read them and react to them. The trick lies in using them and not being carried away by them.

If, for instance, a man you have stopped for questioning is making you angry and nervous, your feelings are telling you that this man is provocative, tense, and possibly dangerous. (If you have not mastered the art of objectivity, your feelings are useless. Your anger might be based as much on the man's color or his resemblance to an in-law you do not like as on his own character.) You should be careful, and you should be aware that attempts to control this man in any way could require assistance. Your own level of fear is often a good measure of when you need help with a situation. You might be thinking about possible cocaine or amphetamine abuse in this man, or scanning pockets, trouser cuffs, belt area, or shirt for weapons. If losing direct eye-contact with this person makes you anxious, you should be unusually cautious and diplomatic. You may recognize his impatience as you begin to feel impatient, and the seconds become longer and longer. If you are running a warrant check, and therefore have a few minutes to kill, you might surreptitiously get a back-up by requesting that someone come by, and then—with the microphone off—add "with a pencil" or "for lunch." Some departments have a special radio code for just such situations to avoid undue provocation or attempts at escape.

All good patrol officers do these things intuitively. Many police officers are good patrol officers. However, others react to their feelings as if those feelings were not a tool but a handicap and an obstacle. They do not enjoy feeling angry, and so they either retreat from patrolling in an active sense or take out their feelings on the supposed source.

To be truly objective is to be rational, and true rationality assumes a balanced experience of one's own emotions. To live one's private life this way might be a bit boring, but to approach work this way is, I feel, constructive. It requires the maturity to withstand thanklessness as much as the maturity to recognize hidden or silent expressions of gratitude. It requires a lot of peer and supervisory support, especially during the first formative months and years on the job. And it depends to some extent on a sense that the public thinks a lot of you, looks up to you, expects and appreciates good work, and rewards your efforts with respect and pay.

It is clear that policing as a profession has its work cut out for it before a working assumption of professional conduct can evolve in its members. Many elements are there—the great responsibility of the job; the trust invested in officers; the idealized expectancies of the public; advances in police science and technology; increasingly high standards for promotion and admission; an increasing acceptance of innovative administration, research, and training—but many are missing. Pride is tarnished and defensive. Self-consciousness comes across as touchiness. And objectivity is learned as a survival attitude on the street rather than as part of an occupational identity to be nurtured and developed from the officer's first day in the academy.

Nothing could advance the profession faster than a radical shift in attitude on the part of police administrators. What the public will withhold until it sees fit to bestow, high-level administrators can often dispense now. That is, they can raise esteem by raising admission standards while making their "moral" yardsticks more flexible. They can short-circuit much griping and juvenility by dumping paramilitary command systems in favor of more mature and effective organizational schemes. They can develop standards for promotion based on supervisory and peer review and experience, as well as clever performance on paper-and-pencil tests. They can withdraw current pseudo-academic education and training and initiate programs based on apprenticeship and role-modeling as well as relevant classroom instruction. Instructors (especially non-police) should realize that they are facing a group of people who, however neatly groomed and orderly, are doers, not sitters. They, like anyone else, cannot be expected to appreciate abstractions in a vacuum. An integrated and well-planned street exposure is essential from the beginning if interest is to be maintained.

I find myself at this point on the verge of filling up paragraph after paragraph of recommendations and exhortations, many of which would be impassioned, and most of which would reveal my admitted bias against present modes of administration in, at least, the department of my experience. Were I to follow this impulse, I would rewrite this book without realizing it. Much of what has been said about discretion, the police function, pressures, and professional "laxity" contains implied criticism of the present state of the craft, and contains simultaneously my faith and trust that police officers will continue to objectify and perfect their work.

I hope that administrators will be more objective in their assessment of my evaluations than I have been in my assessment of their contributions. In the final analysis, policing will advance or regress on the shoulders of the patrol officer. But it appears that only high level police administrators are in a position to substitute strong and progressive professional ideals for the onus of pressure and triviality currently loaded on the patrolman's back.

Notes

1 — THE CONTEXT OF POLICING

1. Albert J. Reiss, Jr. points out that legal institutions, such as appellate courts, formally restrict police authority in the absence of such customs. *The Police and the Public* (New Haven: Yale University Press, 1971), p. 215.
2. William Westley observes that the policeman's need to distinguish, for example, "the better class of people" from "slum dwellers" does not imply that he thinks more highly of one group than the other. *Violence and the Police: A Sociological Study of Law, Custom, and Morality* (Cambridge: MIT Press, 1970), pp. 97–99.
3. Michael Banton notes that "an aggressive middle- or upper-class woman ... is the sort of citizen the police officers least like dealing with, and such incidents require all their tact." *The Policeman in the Community* (New York: Basic Books, 1964), p. 81.
4. Reiss concurs, stating that "strong institutionalized norms support both aggression and violence on the part of citizens as well as suspicion or hostility toward police intervention." Reiss, op. cit., p. 2. See also Egon Bittner, *The Functions of the Police in Modern Society: A Review of Background Factors, Current Practices, and Possible Role Models* (Washington, D.C.: U.S. Government Printing Office, 1970). Bittner notes in Chapter 2 that because policemen are required to deal with matters involving subtle human conflicts and profound legal and moral questions without being allowed to

149

give the subtleties and profundities anywhere near the considera-
tion they deserve, their activities often are invested with the character of crudeness.

5. Charles B. Saunders notes that Americans often feel negatively
toward police authority not only because police seem to represent a
threat to individualistic values, but also because a good many people
subscribe to the stereotype of the head-cracking "dumb-cop," unfortunately confirmed in decades past. *Upgrading the American
Police: Education and Training for Better Law Enforcement* (Washington, D.C.: The Brookings Institution, 1970), Chapter 2. Witness
the reaction of an elderly neighbor to the news that I was becoming a
policeman: "What? All that education just to go out and hit people
over the head?!" See also Jerome Skolnick, *Justice Without Trial*
(New York: John Wiley and Sons, 1966), especially Chapter 1.

6. This subjective estimate by police of the public feeling toward them
stands in contrast to the results of several surveys showing the
public to be far more sympathetic than police realize. For example,
a survey of three precincts in Washington, D.C., made by the Bureau
of Social Science Research found that 60% of those questioned
thought the police had a high reputation in their neighborhood;
85% thought that the police deserve more thanks than they get; 68%
thought that the police should get more pay; and 78% thought
that "just a few policemen . . . are responsible for the bad publicity."
The President's Commission on Law Enforcement and Administration of Justice, "Salient Findings on Crime and Attitudes Toward
Law Enforcement in the District of Columbia," *Task Force Report:
The Police* (Washington, D.C.: U.S. Government Printing Office,
1967), pp. 145–146. My own feeling is that these surveys fall victim to the usual faults of questionnaire surveys, i.e., superficiality
and lack of substance. Thus, for example. "In-depth interviews with
members of minority groups frequently lead to strong statements of
hostility, replacing the neutral or even favorable statements which
began the interview. . . . The way in which such hostility can become
an important factor in a riot is illustrated by the following statement
of a resident of Watts to an interviewer: 'Two white policemen was
beating a pregnant colored lady like a damn dog. They need their
heads knocked off. I agree 100 percent for the Negroes going crazy—
they should have killed those freaks. Yes, treating niggers like dirty
dogs.' This incident, which was thought by many people in Watts to
have been the cause of the 1965 L.A. riot, never occurred. But many
Negroes apparently were prepared to believe that police officers act
in such an improper manner." Ibid., pp. 147–148. In America, a certain amount of good feeling toward "our brave defenders of the
public peace," most evident in public outpourings of sympathy when
an officer is killed in the line of duty, obscures the simultaneous

truth that we do not consider police worthy of our day-to-day trust and support in their more mundane duties.

7. "The extent to which contact (between police and citizens) affects attitudes is a product, at least in part, of the sensitivity of the respondent's relations with the police. . . . For (non-minorities) contact is uninformative; it does not cause them to reevaluate the police, because they are not particularly sensitized to the relationship. But Negroes do not enter or walk away from contact with the police indifferently. On the contrary, it is terribly significant for them, and they learn from it." D. Bayley and H. Mendelsohn, *Minorities and the Police: Confrontation in America* (New York: The Free Press, 1969), p. 67.

8. However, see Elaine Cumming, Ian Cumming, and Laura Edell, "Policeman as Philosopher, Guide, and Friend," *Social Problems,* Volume 12, No. 3, pp. 276–286. The authors observe the sincere, if sentimental, concern policemen have toward children.

9. In survey interviews with officers in high-crime-rate precincts of Boston, Chicago, and Washington, D.C., Reiss found that 80% of all officers thought juveniles were harder to deal with "now than formerly"—almost double the percentage for dealing with "people in his precinct." Reiss observes, correctly, that "harassment will become police policy or unofficial practice whenever citizen influence compels the police to make arrests that are systematically disregarded by others in the criminal justice system." This applies to juveniles, minorities, and those engaged in vice under certain conditions. Reiss, op. cit., pp. 137–138.

10. This phrase is taken from an editorial on the police role in the Detroit riots in the summer of 1967 (*New York Times,* July 27, 1967), and expresses the predicament of police so well that a retired New York City police lieutenant made it the title of his book. See Herbert Klein, *The Police: Damned If They Do—Damned If They Don't* (New York: Crown Publishers, Inc., 1968). Lieutenant Klein's book is full of conservative despair over our declining civilization, but whether or not we agree with such feelings, we should see why they have so much appeal for many police officers.

11. Saunders observes that continued erosion of the authority of schools, churches, the family, and other institutions of social control leaves the law enforcement agencies to deal alone with some of society's deepest problems. Saunders, op. cit., Chapter 6.

12. Milton Rokeach, M. Miller, and J. Snyder, "The Value Gap Between Police and Policed," *Journal of Social Issues,* Volume 27, No. 2, 1971, p. 155. There is some doubt, which Rokeach recognizes, as to whether the low value placed on equality is a result of the job or is present in the applicant prior to his working as a policeman.

2 — THE POLICE FUNCTION

1. "By adopting a 'let sleeping dogs lie' approach, the administrator avoids a direct confrontation and thus is able to support 'effective' practices without having to decide whether they meet the requirements of law." The President's Commission on Law Enforcement and Administration of Justice, *Task Force Report: The Police* (Washington, D.C.: U.S. Government Printing Office, 1969), p. 78.
2. "Americans are a people used to entrusting the solution of their social ills to specialists, and to expecting results from the institutions those specialists devise. They have entrusted the problems of crime to the police, forgetting that they still operate with many of the limitations of constables of years past, even though today's citizens are no longer villagers." Ibid., p. 2.
3. "For (law-abiding citizens who live in a law-abiding community) the phenomenon of crime seems far simpler than in fact it is. The voluntary controls of society work well for them and, since they have no desire to violate the criminal law, their supposition is that crime must be a choice between right and wrong for all men, and that more effective policing alone can determine this choice. Thus public concern about crime is typically translated into demands for more law enforcement, and often into making the police scapegoats for a crime problem they did not create and do not have the resources to solve." Ibid.
4. James Q. Wilson points out that the characterization of police as primarily crime fighters places them in a potentially embarrassing situation, that of being judged by a goal they cannot attain. Their reaction in such a dilemma is actually quite predictable—they lie. Records are "adjusted" so as to give the public the idea that "cases" are being "cleared" and arrests are keeping pace with growing crime rates. Even the "crime rate" itself is subject to statistical manipulation. "The Dilemma of The Urban Police," *The Atlantic*, Vol. 228, No. 3 (March 1969), pp. 129–135.
5. "Even experienced police officers, such as the late Chief of the Los Angeles Police Department, William H. Parker, resist attempts to make them more conscious of human relations problems by arguing that policemen are not agents of social welfare and adjustment. Policemen, in this view, must be deployed according to criminal effects, not criminal causes. . . . What is generally not perceived, or admitted, is that in meeting this obligation, policemen daily engage in activities designed to prevent unambiguously criminal situations from arising and to ameliorate stressful circumstances." Bayley and Mendelsohn, op. cit., p. 78.
6. "Policemen, especially patrolmen, spend most of their time interceding and rendering assistance in nonpunitive ways. They interrupt behavior many more times than they punish it." Ibid., p. 69.

7. Egon Bittner observes that because the idea that the police are basically a crime fighting agency has never been challenged in the past, no one has ever bothered to sort out the remaining priorities. Instead, the police have always been forced to justify activities that did not involve law enforcement in the direct sense by either linking them constructively to law enforcement or by defining them as nuisance demands for service. Bittner, op. cit., p. 4.
8. Bayley and Mendelsohn, op. cit., p. 57.
9. Bittner, op. cit., p. 81.

3 — POLICE DISCRETION

1. See The President's Commission on Law Enforcement and Administration of Justice, *Task Force Report: The Police*, 1967, pp. 19–20. Also, H. Goldstein, "Police Discretion: The Ideal vs. The Real," *Public Administration Review*, Vol. 23 (September 1963), pp. 142–143.
2. "Social control . . . is a property of states of social relations, not something imposed from outside. The level of control, be it high or low, is determined by the kinds of social relationships that exist among the individuals who make up the society, and their effectiveness in getting people to follow prescribed patterns of behavior." Banton, op. cit., p. 2.
3. Jesse Rubin, "Police Identity and the Police Role," in Robert F. Steadman (ed.), *The Police and the Community* (Baltimore: The Johns Hopkins University Press, 1972), p. 19.
4. "On all personality scales the data show that policemen are absolutely average people, and when they do differ from the community norm, it is in the direction of being better or more nobly disposed than their fellowmen. We find no evidence that particular personality types are recruited to police work." Bayley and Mendelsohn, op. cit., p. 15.
5. J.D. Matarazzo, B.V. Allen, G. Saslow, and A.N. Wiens, "Characteristics of Successful Policemen and Firemen Applicants," *Journal of Applied Psychology*, 48, 1964, pp. 123–133.
6. J. Block and P. Peterson, "Q-sort item analysis of a number of Strong Vocational Interest Inventory scales," *Technical Memorandum OERL-TM-55-9* (Officer Education Research Laboratory, Air Force Personnel and Training Research Center, Air Research and Development Command, Maxwell Air Force Base, Alabama, May 1955). Also, H.G. Gough, M.G. McKee, and R.J. Yandell, "Adjective Check List Analyses of a Number of Selected Psychometric and Assessment Variables," ibid.
7. Robert Hogan, "A Study of Police Effectiveness," *Experimental Publication System*, Issue No. 6, Manuscript No. 195c (Washington, D.C.: American Psychological Association, June 1970).

8. Hogan, "The Development of an Empathy Scale,"*Journal of Consulting and Clinical Psychology,* 33, 1969, pp. 307–316.
9. Hogan, "A Study of Police Effectiveness," op. cit.
10. Rokeach, Miller, and Snyder, op. cit., pp. 155–171.
11. Ibid., p. 164.
12. J. Goldstein, "Police Discretion Not to Invoke the Criminal Process: Low-visibility Decisions in the Administration of Justice," *Yale Law Journal,* 69, 1960, p. 543.
13. Bittner, "The Police on Skid Row: A Study of Peacekeeping," *American Sociological Review,* 32 (October 1967), pp. 699–715.
14. Bittner points out that all police departments employ some officers who like to harass people solely on the basis of their own gratuitous fascination with power, and tend to assign these officers disproportionately to districts populated by alienated and powerless people. But by the same token, "My own experience leads me to think that they are probably not more numerous than cruel teachers." *The Functions of the Police in Modern Society,* op. cit., pp. 99–100. In other research Bittner noted that "The explicit refusal to answer questions of a personal nature and the demand to know why the questions are asked significantly enhance a person's chances of being arrested on some minor charge. While most patrolmen tend to be personally indignant about this kind of response and use the arrest to compose their own hurt feelings, this is merely a case of affect being in line with the method. There are other officers who proceed in the same manner without taking offense, or even with feelings of regret. Such patrolmen often maintain that their colleagues' affective involvement is a corruption of an essentially valid technique. The technique is oriented to the goal of maintaining operational control." Bittner, "The Police on Skid Row," op. cit. My own observations suggest that there may be dynamically (in the psychological sense) different reasons for the use of this technique by individual patrolmen, and that the technique itself may only be used in specific situations, as when a new officer is in the process of "proving himself" in a new neighborhood, or when the reticent citizen may be involved in some major criminal activity but must be arrested on more petty grounds for a less serious offense because there is not sufficient basis (yet) for a felony arrest of the person. If an officer arrested every person who was rude to him in a tour of duty, he would spend all his off-duty hours in court!
15. "When an arrest is made, complex personal interactions come into play. The definition of 'criminal' is not based so much on behavior in obvious violation of a specific criminal law as it is on circumstances present in the encounter between policeman and suspect." Richard Quinney, Ed., *Crime and Justice in Society* (Boston: Little, Brown and Co., 1969), p .119. Quinney observes further that

the probabilistic model that police use to judge others' intentions makes the outward appearance of suspects very important.

16. See Rubin, op. cit., pp. 37–39 for a discussion of the conflicts of the black officer.

17. Westley observed the "reality shock" experienced by recruits in their first encounters with the public. "Thus the stories and instruction that he received from his older partners, which he first held only as logical constructs, as reasonable positions, deepen and become empowered with the emotional force of bitter experience." Westley, op. cit., p. 160; also, pp. 73–76. Arthur Niederhoffer has conceptualized a schema of progressive "stages" of cynicism through which an officer travels from the academy to retirement. *Behind the Shield: The Police in Urban Society* (Garden City, New York: Anchor Books, 1969), p. 104.

18. Bittner notes that policemen who use too much or too little force, or whose exercise of force is determined primarily by personal feelings rather than situational exigencies, are considered poor craftsmen by their colleagues. "The Police on Skid Row," op. cit.

4 — THE PRESSURES OF POLICING

1. James F. Ahern, *Police in Trouble* (New York: Hawthorne Books, Inc., 1972).

2. Westley, op. cit., p. xvii.

3. Bayley and Mendelsohn, op. cit., p. 15.

4. Ibid., p. 7.

5. In contrasting British and American police, Banton observes that "Often the American officer views his occupational role simply as a job and, either because of the national culture or because of frustrating elements in the way the department is run, he is not particularly dedicated to the duties of the role." Banton, op. cit., p. 219.

6. Bayley and Mendelsohn account for the observed conservativism of police officers by pointing to factors in the selection process whereby police departments screen applicants, as well as to factors inherent in the job, i.e., order-maintenance, regularity, etc. Yet lest anyone equate conservativism with authoritarianism, the authors point out that Denver police officers (the city of their study) scored lower on a scale of authoritarianism than the general populations of Nashville, Tenn. and Lansing, Mich. Bayley and Mendelsohn, op. cit., p. 17.

7. William Kroes has devoted a readable and insightful volume to the discussion of stress in police work, and suggests other ways of classifying stress. *Society's Victim—the Policeman: An Analysis of*

Job Stress in Policing (Springfield, Ill.: Charles C. Thomas, Publisher, 1976).

8. "The relatively low prestige of police work, the fact that police chiefs have to persuade local government bodies of the need for funds (and other matters) contribute to the tendency for police departments to be seen as business organizations which must justify themselves in the public's eyes." Banton, op. cit., p. 236.

9. Ahern, op. cit., Chapter 3. Ahern says that since very few rewards are available in police work, punishment is the only form of control available. Departmental rules, therefore, virtually assure that if a supervisor does not like someone beneath him, he can "legitimately" discipline him for some petty infraction.

10. See Jonathan Rubinstein, *City Police* (New York: Farrar, Straus, and Giroux, 1973), pp. 441-442, for an example of "rookie-testing" on this score.

11. The men were in a special "operations" car, not a regularly assigned "beat" car. A beat car would never have the time for such a trip. Operations cars were allowed more flexibility in patrolling but were expected to stay strictly in their assigned areas. They were also expected to back up regular patrol officers on hazardous calls, issue traffic and parking tickets, make bank and business checks, and handle any "on view" calls from citizens who approached them. They were, in effect, freed from primary responsibility for handling routine calls for service and traffic accidents, unless they happened on the scene prior to the assignment of the accident to a beat car.

12. As Ahern observes, "An entire book could be written on the excuses cops give for being where they are not supposed to be." Ahern, op. cit., Chapter 1.

13. Rubinstein, op. cit., pp. 129–130.

14. There is nothing magic about the five-year mark. The competence of some officers is recognized earlier, and that of others is occasionally never recognized. But for purposes of generalization, it is often believed that at least five years' experience is necessary to train a radio car patrolman. Bruce Smith, *Police Systems in the United States* (New York: Harper and Row, 1960), p. 114.

15. Bittner has coined an elegant definition of the police role which includes what appears to be the concept of "common sense": "The role of the police is best understood as a mechanism for the distribution of non-negotiably coercive force, employed in accordance with the dictates of an intuitive grasp of situational exigencies." *The Functions of the Police in Modern Society*, p. 46.

16. Bittner, "The Police on Skid Row," pp. 699–715.

17. Rubinstein, op. cit., pp. 81–82.

18. Peter B. Bloch and Deborah Anderson, *Policewoman on Patrol: Final Report* (Washington, D.C.: Police Foundation, 1974). Reported in *Time*, May 27, 1974, p. 8.

19. "Every policeman is faced at some point with the temptation to beat a prisoner. There is always someone who angers him or arouses a fear in him that he seeks to eradicate by punishing the person who caused him to quiver." Rubinstein, op. cit., p. 321.

20. E. M. Colbach and C. D. Fosterling, *Police Social Work* (Springfield, Ill.: Charles C. Thomas, Publisher, 1976), pp. 119–123.

21. Kroes, op. cit., p. 88. Kroes sees this "deadening of affect" as part of the officer's physiological adaptation to stress.

22. Bayley and Mendelsohn offer an interesting list of "minority" attributes applicable to police officers:
    1) They are thought of in stereotypes.
    2) They present a uniform appearance to non-police.
    3) They have a low status in the community that is incongruent with their high self-image.
    4) They are regularly treated to verbal and physical abuse.
    5) They are convinced that they are systematically misunderstood.
    6) They are conscious of being portrayed in the media in a simplistic, detracting manner.
    7) They live in an environment of attitudes that seems quixotic and uncertain.
    8) They are respected in principle but not in fact, and are expected to know their place and not be too pushy or offensive.
    9) In search of support, they turn inward on their own families and colleagues. They fear that people outside their community cannot be relied on to be fair and impartial.
    Bayley and Mendelsohn, op. cit., p. 54.

23. Kroes, op. cit., p. 60.

24. Ahern, op. cit., Chapter 1.

5 — STYLES OF POLICING

1. James Q. Wilson, *Varieties of Police Behavior: The Management of Law and Order in Eight Communities* (Cambridge, Mass.: Harvard University Press, 1968).

2. Melany Baehr studied the characteristics and performances of Chicago police officers, and, using a statistical technique known as "nodal analysis," distinguished eight different styles or levels of performance based on a number of psychological tests and behavioral ratings. These styles are in substantial agreement with my own observations concerning individual styles of policing. See Melany Baehr, *Psychological Assessment of Patrolman Qualifications in Relation to Field Performance* (Washington, D.C.: U.S. Government Printing Office, 1968).

3. "The most eminent of modern police administrators, August Vollmer, once said: 'I have spent my life enforcing the laws. It is

a stupid procedure and has not, nor will it ever solve the problem unless it is supplemented by preventive measures.'" *Task Force Report: The Police,* 1967, p. 2.

4. "Because patrolmen perceive military discipline as degrading, ornery, and unjust, the only motive they have for doing well is to get out of the uniformed assignments. Therefore, patrol suffers from a constant drain of ambitious and enterprising men. In consequence, the outward appearance of patrol hides a great deal of discontent, demoralization, and marginal work quality." Bittner, *The Functions of the Police in Modern Society,* Chapter 8.

5. It should be mentioned at this point that in the eyes of patrol officers, there is only a fleeting satisfaction involved in the apprehension of a felon. It is a common belief that courts are so lenient, and prisons so inept at reform, that the criminal is likely to be back on the streets in a relatively short time, having learned little but a firmer desire to resist apprehension and incarceration in the future. This of course makes any police contact with the released "felon" all the more hazardous.

6. *Task Force Report: The Police,* 1967, p. 53.

7. Richard Harris, *The Police Academy: An Inside View* (New York: John Wiley & Sons, Inc., 1973).

8. For further insight into the subtle reciprocity of the sergeant-patrolman relation, see Rubinstein, op. cit., pp. 37–43, 56–57, 114–115, 448–452.

9. For an example of this, see ibid., p. 53.

10. In *Upgrading the American Police,* p. 85, Saunders cites some evidence that college-educated officers become frustrated and dissatisfied, and eventually leave police work. A patrol instructor in the police academy warned our class as a group that in his experience college-educated recruits did not last on the street. The almost explicit message was that people with college degrees are too "soft" or "egg-heady" to endure the rough nature of street policing. The irony here is that this instructor was forced out of street patrol by a serious ulcer, and was diligently pursuing his B.A. degree at nights in a local college! That there may well be some distinct differences between college-educated police and non-college-educated police is indicated by a study which concludes that "Police who are attracted to college are significantly less authoritarian than police who are not impelled to attend college." Smith, Locke, and Warner, "Authoritarianism in College and Non-college-Oriented Police,'" *Journal of Criminal Law, Criminology, and Police Science,* Vol. 58 (March 1967), p. 132. The lessons to be learned here are that people often go to different sorts of colleges for different reasons, and that any stereotyping of "college-educated" police is likely to be as inadequate as most other stereotyping. Research in this area will obviously have to be careful in teasing out the motivations and experiences of col-

lege graduates who seek police careers and police officers who seek college educations.

11. This distaste for the contemplative is also one of the major blocks to substantive and useful police academy training. Says Banton, "Experienced police officers develop very considerable skill in handling different sorts of people but because they acquire it unconsciously and are not given to examination of their own reactions, they usually cannot explain quite how they deal with awkward cases or why they employ one approach rather than another." Banton, op. cit., p. 178. Formal training, therefore, tends to be confined to generalities and exhortation.

6 — NOTES ON PREJUDICE: POLICING THE GHETTO

1. Ed Gray, *The Enemy in the Streets: Police Malpractice in America* (Garden City, New York: Anchor Books, 1972).

2. "Minorities, especially Negroes, in the eyes of police personnel, demand the most, raise the greatest amount of anxiety about personal safety, pose the greatest criminal threat, are the most hostile, and on top of it all are as likely to be truculent in their appeals against officers as prosperous (non-Minorities). . . . One can understand why policemen often show a sense of being aggrieved, mistreated, and put-upon by minorities. Minorities react in an exactly similar fashion against members of the majority community." Bayley and Mendelsohn, op. cit., p. 108.

3. *Task Force Report: The Police,* 1967, p. 148.

4. See James Q. Wilson, "The Police in the Ghetto," in Steadman, op. cit., pp. 51–97. Wilson picks apart the myth that police and ghetto residents are engaged in a form of warfare, while noting that the high crime rate of lower class males (who in this case happen to be black), the "homogeneity" of appearance blacks give to white officers and vice-versa, and the function of the police itself, regardless of the attitudes of police, all contribute to create a very problematic situation. Rubinstein also notes that actions taken by officers in high-crime areas can be seen as "prejudiced" but actually reflect the reality of life in that area. Rubinstein, op. cit., p. 263. We have yet to determine the best "trade-off" between the benefits of "aggressive patrol" and the damage it does to police-community relations.

5. Bayley and Mendelsohn, op. cit., p. 112.

6. *Task Force Report: The Police,* 1967, p. 148.

7. See Skolnick, op. cit., Chapter 4. Skolnick cautions against assuming that policemen are prejudiced merely because they do not share our fondness for euphemisms in describing societal failures.

8. See Wilson, "The Police in the Ghetto," pp. 64–66, for some statistical confirmation of this.

9. "The policeman, because his work requires him to be occupied continually with potential violence, develops a perceptual shorthand to identify certain kinds of people as symbolic assailants, i.e., as persons who use gesture, language, and attire that the policeman has come to recognize as a prelude to violence." Skolnick, op. cit., p. 45.

10. See Irving Piliavin and Scott Briar, "Police Encounters with Juveniles," *American Journal of Sociology,* 70 (September 1964), pp. 206–214.

11. Rubinstein, op. cit., p. 98.

12. The police department in which I worked has an "Officer Friendly" program in which uniformed community relations officers visit public elementary schools in an effort to break down the stereotypes of fear and mistrust of police that develop in black youngsters. The children are urged to wave and say hello to officers they see on the street, and officers almost always respond in kind.

13. Rubinstein, op. cit., p. 151.

14. See Bittner, "The Police on Skid Row," pp. 699–715.

7— NOTES TO SOCIAL SCIENTISTS, ESPECIALLY PSYCHOLOGISTS

1. Martin Reiser maintains that a psychologist-consultant (in-house) should be "connected" to the police department at the highest levels possible. In this way he can have maximum effect on the important decisions made by a department, and can be in the best possible position to have his own ideas accepted and implemented. *The Police Department Psychologist* (Springfield, Illinois: Charles C. Thomas, 1972), pp. 12, 47. Because Reiser also stresses the importance of regular contacts with line officers, his overall view of the consultant's role vis-a-vis the departmental power structure is a balanced one. However, it reflects ideal conditions of management-line relations that may not exist in many large urban departments. In conflict-ridden departments, the psychologist-consultant will have the very delicate job of communicating with line and administration personnel without being trapped into proselytizing for one "side" or the other. Whether this can indeed be done remains to be seen. It is obvious that my own experience reflects substantial suspicion of high-level administrators and their feelings about organizational subordinates. Consultants can thus be forewarned against thoroughgoing identification with any one segment of the department, regardless of any seeming "correctness" in the identification.

2. Rubinstein, op. cit.

3. Ibid., p. 417.

4. Colbach and Fosterling, op. cit.

8 — NOTES TO POLICE:
AN EDITORIAL ON ETHICS

1. Ahern, op. cit.
2. Lincoln Steffens, *The Shame of the Cities* (New York: McClure, Phillips, 1904).
3. There is, however, some analogy between police accused of abuse and doctors accused of malpractice. This lies in shared feelings of being themselves abused by the system of redress, with the result that as police are now demanding the right to confront their accusers in an open hearing, so too doctors are beginning to countersue their accusers when malpractice claims are made frivolously.
4. *Task Force Report: The Police,* 1967, p. 213.
5. Herman Goldstein, *Police Corruption: A Perspective on its Nature and Control* (Washington, D.C.: The Police Foundation, 1975), p. 52. After a concise review of corruption in its many shapes and forms, Professor Goldstein concludes that police administrators have the difficult but necessary task of controlling the inevitable corruption that will surface within their departments. He then suggests some courses an administrator might follow and warns of the associated pitfalls. My thought on this subject is the more optimistic one that as administrators work toward improving the quality of their officers and the sophistication of their training and work, corruption will diminish largely of its own accord. I look for the solution, in other words, to come from within the officer rather than from administratively imposed controls.

Index